OUR JEWISH HERITAGE

Other books by Joseph Gaer

THE BIBLE FOR FAMILY READING
(a new version; in collaboration with Dr. Chester C. McCown)

THE LORE OF THE OLD TESTAMENT *(Biblical Folklore)*

THE LORE OF THE NEW TESTAMENT *(Apocryphal Folklore)*

THE UNCONQUERED *(Biblical Folklore)*

THE BURNING BUSH *(Biblical Folklore)*

THE MAGIC FLIGHT *(Jewish Folk Tales)*

HOW THE GREAT RELIGIONS BEGAN

YOUNG HEROES OF THE LIVING RELIGIONS

HOLIDAYS AROUND THE WORLD
(Religious holidays and festivals)

THE FABLES OF INDIA *(from some of the Sacred Books of India)*

THE ADVENTURES OF RAMA
(a children's version of the Hindu epic Ramayana)

THE WISDOM OF THE LIVING RELIGIONS

THE LEGEND CALLED MERYOM *(a novel)*

HEART UPON THE ROCK *(a novel)*

and others

OUR
JEWISH
HERITAGE

BY

JOSEPH GAER

and

RABBI ALFRED WOLF

Illustrated with Photographs

HENRY HOLT AND COMPANY

NEW YORK

PREFACE

In the course of a lifetime one is apt to be asked many times, "What are you?" And we are likely to give a variety of answers. For we are many things.

First of all, and most important, we are human beings. And if we are *good* human beings, that is all that really matters. Then, human beings are members of a given nation and citizens of a given country. To the question, "What are you?" we might answer, "I am a Frenchman," or "I am an Englishman," or "I am a Pakistani," or any one of the many nationalities in the world. We also have vocations that distinguish us one from another. To the question, "What are you?" we might answer, "I am a teacher," or "I am a preacher," or "I am a mechanic," or any one of the many different occupations and professions. We might even identify ourselves by our avocations, as golfers, or big-game hunters or archers or philatelists.

Next only to being a human being, the important answer to the question, "What are you?" concerns itself with one's faith. We might belong to any of the world's great religions, or to an obscure group that does not even claim to be a religion but calls itself an ethical or mystical society.

In this book we are concerned with a rather small segment of mankind, but one whose influence in human history is universally acknowledged, and whose members answer the question, "What are you?" with "I am a Jew."

What is a Jew? Who is a Jew? What does a Jew believe? What does a Jew do because he is a Jew? Which holidays does

he celebrate and why? How does he pray, and what does he
pray for? What is his daily regimen and what are his traditional practices on life's most important occasions? How does
his history affect his religion? How do his religion and history affect his way of life? What are the various forms of Judaism that exist in America today? And what are their differences? The answer to these and other related questions are
given here in their simplest form.

We Jews are a very old people. Our religion and our way of
life have evolved and constantly changed over a period of
more than four thousand years. During these many centuries
the adherents of Judaism have developed a number of attitudes as well as traits. These attitudes and traits are subtle
and complex, and they cannot be grasped unless people know,
first, the general nature of Judaism, the religion, and, second,
the Jewish heritage, which is principally religious.

Here our primary attention is given to Judaism as a religion in practice, and to what the Jewish heritage represents.
It is intended as a primer to introduce to those not conversant
with the topic the theory and practice of Judaism, and the
principles and precepts of this faith.

We are profoundly indebted to the following organizations and publishers for permission to quote from the books listed below and bearing
their imprint:

Bloch Publishing Company, American publishers of *The Authorized
Daily Prayer Book,* edited by Dr. Joseph H. Hertz (Orthodox);

The Central Conference of American Rabbis, publishers of *The
Union Prayerbook for Jewish Worship* and the *Union Haggadah* (Reform);

The Hebrew Publishing Company, publishers of the *Service of the
Synagogue: New Year and Day of Atonement;* and *Festival Services for
Passover, Feast of Weeks and Tabernacles,* edited by H. M. Adler, Israel
Zangwill, Arthur Davis, and Nina Salaman (Orthodox);

The Jewish Welfare Board, whose imprint appears on *The Haggadah
of Passover* by David and Tamar de Sola Pool;

Little, Brown & Company, publishers of *The Bible for Family Reading*, prepared by Joseph Gaer, from which The Book of Esther is quoted;

The Reconstructionist Press, publishers of the *Sabbath Prayer Book; High Holiday Prayer Book,* Volumes I and II;

Behrman House, Inc., publishers of *The New Haggadah* by Mordecai M. Kaplan, Eugene Kohn and Ira Eisenstein (Reconstructionist);

United Synagogue of America, whose *Sabbath and Festival Prayer Book* and *High Holiday Prayer Book,* edited by Rabbi Morris Silverman, are published by the Prayer Book Press (Conservative).

We are even more deeply indebted to several scholars for their generosity and kindness in reading this book in manuscript and in galleys and for allowing us to benefit greatly by their perceptive comments and suggestions. They are: Dr. Samuel S. Cohon, Professor Emeritus of the Hebrew Union College, who gave so much of his time in a careful reading of the manuscript and a detailed criticism; Dr. Simon Greenberg, Vice-Chancellor of the Jewish Theological Seminary, whose *The Conservative Movement in Judaism* served as the basis for our treatment of that section in our book, and who read the manuscript before it went to press; Rabbi Simon A. Dolgin, scholarly Rabbi of Beth Jacob Congregation in Los Angeles, who read the manuscript with close attention both for accuracy of statement and its literary impact; Rabbi Edgar F. Magnin and Rabbi Maxwell H. Dubin of Wilshire Boulevard Temple in Los Angeles who read and commented on the book in manuscript; and we are particularly grateful to Dr. Abraham E. Millgram, Educational Director of The United Synagogue Commission of Jewish Education, whose constructive criticism of the manuscript and suggestions for the order of the contents have helped strengthen the book.

Joseph Gaer and
Alfred Wolf

May 23, 1957

CONTENTS

PART I

ON BEING A JEW

"You shall love your neighbor as yourself."
—Leviticus 19:18

WHO IS A JEW?

FOR THE DESCRIPTION and explanation of the Jewish heritage it seems necessary first to define what we mean by the term "Jew." In spite of the long history of the Jewish people, or because of it, a number of misconceptions cling to the term which blur or even conceal the image it should invoke.

Often a person is described as belonging to the Jewish *race*. Yet there is no such thing as a Jewish race.

If we go back to the days of Abraham, Isaac, and Jacob, the Jews were descendants of a Semitic group to which belonged the ancient Babylonians, the Assyrians, the Phoenicians, and several other Canaanite peoples and many Arab nations. These Semites were not a race in the anthropological sense, since their kinship was that of similarity of language rather than physical characteristics. The term "Semite" is a cultural designation.

Even if "Semite" were a term for a distinct race, many centuries have passed since the Patriarch Abraham came out of the Land of Ur, and his descendants have gone through great migrations and dispersions, during which they have accumulated the progeny of every conceivable racial stock from among the strangers who lived in their midst and in whose midst they lived. Today there is a remnant of Jews in Ethiopia as dark as any in that land. The few Jews in China who have lived there for a number of centuries are yellow-skinned like the Chinese, and their eyes are almond-shaped and slanted. The Jews of India resemble the Hindus, while many of them in the Western world are blond, white-skinned, and have greenish-gray eyes. The language of the

3

Chinese Jew is Chinese; of the French Jew, French; and in England and in the United States the language of the Jew is English. Few third-generation Jews in any country can be readily distinguished by their features and language from the people of the land. Clearly a Jew is not a Jew because of his race.

Sometimes a person is described as belonging to the Jewish *nation*.

This, too, is very confusing. In the days of the Judges the Jews were a group of tribes. In the time of Saul, of David, and of Solomon they were united into a nation. After that period they divided into the two kingdoms of Judah and of Israel. Later the two Jewish kingdoms were destroyed and the people dispersed to the four corners of the earth. After that, and until 1948, there was no Jewish nation. Wherever Jews live, whether native-born or naturalized, to that nation they belong. In 1948 the State of Israel came into being, and her citizens are called Israelis. Not all Israelis are Jews; some are Christians, Moslems, and Hindus. And Jews anywhere in the world, except in Israel, are obviously not Israelis. For Jewishness is not a nationality.

Less deceptive but at times almost as confusing are the terms "Children of Israel" and "Hebrews."

The people who were known as Hebrews trace their descent to Abraham, Isaac, and Jacob. Jacob was renamed Israel (Genesis 32:28), and from his twelve sons issued the twelve tribes who were called the Children of Israel. To them, according to the Bible, was bequeathed the Promised Land, which was named the Land of Israel. And the land and the Hebrew people were considered inseparable. The Children of Israel in the Land of Israel spoke Hebrew and gathered the Sacred Books in that language. Nowadays, the term "Hebrew" usually refers to the language rather than the people.

After the Babylonian exile, the people became known as

Jews, a term originally derived from "Judah," the southern-most tribe of the Children of Israel; and the term was later applied to all people who adhered to Judaism.

And in the term "Jew" we find our clue to its definition: *A Jew is any person who is born into or embraces Judaism.* But Judaism is not a religion in the commonly accepted sense of church adherence, for it is a religion intertwined with the history of a people, a way of life, a complex of attitudes and ideals.

JUDAISM AS A RELIGION

Judaism, like every other religion, is based upon a number of premises concerning the nature of the universe and its Creator, the relation of man to God, and the relation of man to man, dictated by his concept of the nature of God. Upon these fundamental concepts each religion builds its structure of precepts and commandments which are to regulate behavior. A number of these premises are the same in several religions and ethical systems and are a common bond. But basic differences also exist between religions, and such differences can be traced to the differences in the fundamental articles of faith from which they start.

Many attempts have been made to formalize the basic Judaic principles, or premises, or Articles of Faith. The Jewish philosopher Philo (20 B.C.E.–50 C.E.) * made such an attempt. In his work on Creation he enumerated Five Principles, which were the fundamental concepts of Judaism:

1. The belief in God
2. There is only One God
3. The World was created by Him but is not eternal
4. There is only One universe
5. God cares for the world and all its creatures, as a parent cares for his children

---

* In Jewish literature B.C.E. (Before the Common Era) and C.E. (Common Era) are used instead of B.C. and A.D.

The best-known and generally accepted formalization of the Judaic Articles of Faith was made by Maimonides, or Moses ben Maimon (1135-1204), the great Jewish philosopher who codified Jewish Law. He reduced the Judaic doctrine to Thirteen Principles. Though these were never officially accepted, they were incorporated into the daily Prayerbooks. And these are the Thirteen Principles of Maimonides, the basic credo of Judaism:

1. I believe with perfect faith that the Creator, blessed be His Name, is the Creator and Guide of everything that has been created, and He alone has made, does make, and will make all things.

2. I believe with perfect faith that the Creator, blessed be His Name, is One, and that there is no unity in any manner like unto His, and that He alone is our God, who was, and is, and will be.

3. I believe with perfect faith that the Creator, blessed be His Name, is not a body, and that He is free from all the properties of matter, and that He has not any form whatever.

4. I believe with perfect faith that the Creator, blessed be His Name, is the first and the last.

5. I believe with perfect faith that to the Creator, blessed be His Name, and to Him alone, it is right to pray, and that it is not right to pray to any being beside Him.

6. I believe with perfect faith that all the words of the prophets are true.

7. I believe with perfect faith that the prophecy of Moses, our teacher, peace be unto him, was true, and that he was the chief of the prophets, both of those who preceded and of those who followed him.

8. I believe with perfect faith that the whole Torah, now in our possession, is the same that was given to Moses, our teacher, peace be unto him.

9. I believe with perfect faith that this Torah will not be changed, and that there will never be any other Law from the Creator, blessed be His Name.

10. I believe with perfect faith that the Creator, blessed be His Name, knows every deed of the children of men, and all their thoughts, as it is said, It is He that fashioned the hearts of them all, that gives heed to all their works.

11. I believe with perfect faith that the Creator, blessed be His Name, rewards those that keep His commandments and punishes those that transgress them.

12. I believe with perfect faith in the coming of the Messiah; and, though he tarry, I will wait daily for his coming.

13. I believe with perfect faith that there will be a revival of the dead at the time when it shall please the Creator, blessed be His Name, and exalted be His fame for ever and ever.

For Thy salvation I hope, O Lord.

Here we have the expression of belief in the existence of God, the Creator of all things; Who is the only One, incorporeal and eternal; to Whom alone we must pray; the belief in prophecy of the prophets, of whom Moses was the greatest, and to whom was revealed the Law, which will never be abrogated; the belief that God knows the thoughts and acts of all men and that He rewards the good and punishes the evil; and, finally, the belief in the coming of the Messiah and the resurrection of the dead.

Maimonides established these principles as the test of believers. "When all these principles of faith are in the safe keeping of a man," he wrote, "he then enters into the general body of Israel."

The great majority of Jews accepted these principles and for nearly seven centuries they became the subject of many religious commentaries.

The first distinguishing feature of Judaism as a spiritual system, based upon its Articles of Faith, is in its conception of all life as subject to Moral Law. The foundations of this religion are the Ten Commandments, which contain implied, it is believed, all of Jewish Law. The various repetitions of the Law, the amplifications and interpretations from the Mishna (compiled by Judah Ha-Nasi in the second century c.e.) are extensions of the idea that no man is a law unto himself but must live by Divine Law to serve God and his fellow men.

Some early scholars counted all the statutes, regulations, and precepts in the Five Books of Moses, and discovered that there were 613 precepts in all. The attempt was then made to sift out the most important. One great teacher finally reduced them to six; another to five; and still another to four. The Prophet Micah reduced them to three: "What does the Lord require of you but (1) to do justice, (2) to love mercy, and (3) to walk humbly with your God?" (Micah 6:8). Isaiah reduced them to two: "(1) Keep justice and (2) do righteousness" (Isaiah 56:1); and Habakkuk—to one: "The righteous shall live by his faith" (Habakkuk 2:4).

Other reductions of the Commandments to one central statement quoted in the Talmud are: The Torah was given for the guidance and benefit of all the "generations of man" (cf. Genesis 5:1): and "Love your neighbor as yourself" (Leviticus 19:18). (The Book of Leviticus underscores that the term "neighbor" includes "the stranger who dwells in your midst.") This basic biblical version of the Golden Rule was rephrased by Hillel (30 b.c.e.—10 c.e.): "Do not unto others that which is hateful to you. This is the whole of the Law; all the rest is commentary" (Shabbat 31a).

JUDAISM AND JEWISH HISTORY

The fundamental concepts of Judaism as a monotheistic religion are universal. But there is among them one belief that the Law was revealed to Moses to be transmitted to the Children of Israel, who were chosen to bring God's Law to the nations of the earth. This concept creates a bond between Judaism and the Children of Israel. And this concept of a bond between God and Israel has been developed to include in Judaism the entire history of the Jewish people insofar as it relates to the trials and triumphs for "the sanctification of God's Name." Because of this concept, Judaism as a faith became deeply interwoven with Judaism as a given people's religious history.

Though Judaism as we know it today did not take form until the time of Ezra (444 B.C.E.), when the Jews returned to Palestine from Babylonian captivity, its history, as far as Jews are concerned, begins with Abraham, the father of Israel, and the first man to conceive the idea of one God, and with whom God made an everlasting Covenant. They believe that before that day, back to the Beginning, and ever since that day, to the present, all that has happened, happened according to a Divine plan. The enslavement of the Children of Israel in Egypt and their ultimate emancipation was all according to this plan. And the remembrance of the emancipation from slavery became central in Judaism, an occasion of great celebration for over thirty-five centuries and a constant reminder that "Because you were slaves in the Land of Egypt and I brought you out with a strong hand," Jews must serve the Lord by doing justice and showing mercy to all men.

Moses, the Emancipator, brought the Children of Israel to Sinai, where he received the Ten Commandments for them. According to tradition, the Commandments were first offered to all the other nations of the earth who, each in turn, rejected them for diverse reasons. The Jews accepted them and thereby became the Chosen People—not the people arbitrarily chosen by the Lord, but the people who purposely chose to live by God's Law. "The gates are open for all the righteous on earth, and if any people is favored in the eyes of the Lord, it is so only because He is favored in their eyes, and they are faithful to His Commandments."

From that day on, and throughout the long centuries,

whatever happened to the Children of Israel, for good or for evil, was predicated on their dedication to God's Law and the sanctification of His Name. Their triumphs were a reward for faithfulness; their failures and tribulations were a punishment for unfaithfulness.

In this way crucial events in the life of the Jewish people became directly related to and interwoven with their faith, until one could not be disassociated from the other. Many of the holidays celebrated, many of the traditions established, many of the precepts practiced, grew from the basic principles of the Faith. But the forms by which these principles are expressed were molded by historic events in the life of the Jewish people. Jewish history and Judaism became so fused that they could not be known one apart from the other.

JUDAISM AS A WAY OF LIFE

The major events in Jewish history, whether tragic or joyful, took place because the Jews clung tenaciously to their religion. Though they themselves were willing to introduce, from within, many changes in customs and even concepts to conform with changing times and historic circumstances, they repelled any attempt from without to alter their Faith, and were willing to suffer persecution and martyrdom rather than to submit.

In the course of centuries the Jews evolved a way of life based on their Faith and historic experiences. They traditionally accepted certain ideals as consonant with their religion which became characteristic of their attitudes, their code of behavior. The very ideals became their way of life.

These ideals might be given as: (1) faith, (2) reverence for wisdom, (3) love of justice, (4) yearning for peace, (5) belief in the sacredness of life, (6) joy of living, (7) charity, (8) immortality, (9) the Messianic hope, (10) sacredness of the family, (11) duty to the community, and (12) respect for knowledge.

The Jewish way of life begins with *faith*. "God will help" is an expression used on every occasion. There is a constant and tacit acceptance that nothing happens unless He wills it; that whatever happens is for the good, since it is part of God's plan. When in trouble, the Jew repeats, "Cast your burden upon the Lord and He will sustain you" (Psalm 55:22). Man has nothing and no one to fear but the Lord. "The fear of the Lord is the beginning of wisdom" (Proverbs 1:7).

This is the basis of the reverence for *wisdom* in Jewish tradition. There are more sayings about the value of wisdom, beyond all material wealth, than there are on almost any other topic. And the traditional teaching is that excellence of wisdom is enhanced by the recognition that "All wisdom comes from the Lord" (Ecclesiastes 1:1).

Yet Judaism stresses that man has freedom of choice and bears responsibility for his actions.

Man is ruled by Divinely given Moral Law, which has as its ultimate objective the establishment of *justice* between man and man. Therefore, every legal decision is a moral decision. In the eyes of the law there can be no distinction of persons; and one must forever remember that what the Lord requires is "to do justice."

Next only to justice the Jews honor *peace*. "How beautiful upon the mountains are the feet of him who brings good tidings, who publishes peace!" (Isaiah 52:7). And they look forward with longing toward the time when "all the nations shall beat their swords into plowshares, and their spears into pruning hooks; nation shall not lift up sword against nation, neither shall they learn war any more" (Isaiah 2:4). In his daily prayers the Jew prays for universal peace; and he fervently believes that "The mission of Israel is peace."

The Jewish yearning for peace is related to the belief in

the *sacredness of all life.* In the Talmud it is asserted that the saving of a single life is as if one had saved mankind. Killing any creature, however lowly, for pleasure or wantonly is forbidden. The Jews constantly use the expression "the grief of living things" (*tza-ar ba-ale haim*) to remind themselves that it is sinful to cause pain or grief to any living creature or not to offer help when a creature is in danger.

Jews also believe that life should be lived joyfully. They remind themselves continually that "A merry heart has a continual feast." And they repeat: "Tears may open the gates, but laughter will tear down the very walls."

So interwoven is the belief in *charity* with the life of a Jew that there is practically no occasion in his life, gay or solemn, when it is not incumbent upon him to give, and to give generously. He is exhorted to: "Open wide your hand to your brother, to the needy and to the poor" (Deuteronomy 15:11), and "Say not to your neighbor, 'Go, and come again, and tomorrow I will give,' when you have it with you" (Proverbs 3:28). He is warned, "He who closes his ear to the cry of the poor shall cry out himself, but shall not be heard" (Proverbs 21:17). But "Whoever practices charity and justice is as though he filled the whole world with loving-kindness" (Bab. Talmud, Sukah 49). For "The more charity, the more peace" (Pirke Abot 2:8). So great is this virtue considered that "Even he who is maintained by charity must himself practice charity" (Bab. Talmud, Gittin 7).

In Jewish tradition it is assumed that the human soul is made "in the image of God"; that since God is eternal, the human soul must be immortal, and that when a man's body dies, his soul continues to live. But since God is incorporeal, the human soul must be incorporeal. This has given rise to a great diversity of opinions about "the world to come," "the resurrection of the dead," and immortality.

In addition to "the world to come" (*Olam Habah*), Judaism emphasizes the Golden Age to come in this world, as foretold by the prophets. This concept has been nurtured by Jews generation after generation, and their anticipation of a Golden Age is embodied in the *Messianic hope.* Dr. Joseph Klausner, in his book, *The Messianic Idea in Israel,* clarifies the difference between the nations who record with longing a Golden Age in the past and the Jewish expectation of a Messiah who will establish a Golden Age upon this earth in the future. This anticipation gives to every Jewish approach an attitude of optimism.

Because of Judaism's enthusiastic affirmation of life in this world, its attitude toward marriage and the family has always been unreservedly positive. The *sacredness of the family* in Jewish tradition means much more than obedience of the commandments forbidding adultery and requiring respect for father and mother. It means a strong bond of mutual responsibility—between husband and wife, between parents and children, between brothers and sisters—far beyond legal requirements. This attitude has made the Jewish home the intimate sanctuary of religion; the family, the prime instrument for the transmission of knowledge. Because of it, the Jewish family has stood the test of time. When persecution scattered Jews all over the globe, the sense of loyalty of one son, one brother, one cousin, in a land of freedom often saved an entire family. When in the industrialized twentieth century the divorce rate rose rapidly in most Western countries, the Jewish family resisted the corrosive forces for many years because of its internal strength; for, although Judaism, since Bible times, permitted divorce, the divorce rate remained low.

The importance of the family and the sacredness of the individual life were balanced, in Jewish tradition, by man's *duty to the community.* He who saves one individual life has saved all mankind; for the individual life exists for the sake of mankind. "If I am not for myself, who is for me?" asked Hillel, "but when I am for myself alone, what am I?"

(Pirke Abot I:14). The same sage's precept: "Do not separate yourself from the congregation!" (Pirke Abot II:5) has been accepted as a basic statement of man's duty toward society. The Jewish community is primarily a congregation. All its activities, religious, educational, social, and charitable, spring from and are centered upon the synagogue. The observant Jew fulfills his duty by support of and his participation in these activities. These duties extend to universal causes, beyond parochial limits; for, in its highest sense, the community includes all who are children of the One Father.

The Jewish concept of the community, since the days of the great academies which produced the Talmud, has been essentially democratic. The opinion of the majority prevailed in a decision; and the minority, while given the right to express and record its opinion, was expected to accept the will of the majority.

But above all, Jews extol *knowledge*. Wisdom is from the Lord, but knowledge can be acquired; and it is the duty of man to acquire it. Jews believe that without knowledge there can be no understanding, and without understanding there can be no justice, and without justice there can be no Moral Law, and without Moral Law there can be no Faith.

It is the duty of every person to gain as much knowledge as possible. In talmudic times, it was expected of all who were judges in Israel to know many languages and the sciences of their day. And the Talmud reflects what high regard the rabbis had for all learning. But for the Jew knowledge begins with knowledge of the books that record and contain the Jewish heritage.

BOOKS OF THE JEWISH HERITAGE

The basic books of Judaism have followed an evolutionary development, with the Mosaic Law as their root.

Jewish tradition was long in the making. Fourteen centuries passed between the time Moses received the Ten Commandments (which became the core of Jewish Law) and the time when the Sanhedrin gave final approval to a list of Sacred Books. Among a great number of books the Jewish people had accumulated, tradition rejected many for various theological reasons. Some of these rejected books have since been completely lost and forgotten; some still exist in obscurity and are known as Pseudepigrapha; and fourteen others were preserved in the Greek translation of the Bible and are known as Apocrypha. The twenty-four books finally approved by the Synod in 90 C.E. have ever since been the accepted Hebrew Scriptures.

In Hebrew the Scriptures are divided in three parts: the Torah (the Five Books of Moses); the Prophets; and the Sacred Writings:

1. The Torah, often called the Law or Five Books of Moses: namely, Genesis, Exodus, Leviticus, Numbers, and Deuteronomy.

2. *Nevi'im,* or the Prophets, which are divided into two groups: the Early Prophets (Joshua, Judges, Samuel, and Kings) and the Later Prophets (Isaiah, Jeremiah, Ezekiel, and the twelve books of the "minor" prophets).

3. *K'tuvim,* or Sacred Writings (not included with the Law and the Prophets), which contain the Psalms, Proverbs, Job, Song of Songs, Ruth, Ecclesiastes, Esther, Daniel, Ezra, Nehemiah, and the Chronicles.

The most sacred part of the Scriptures is the Torah; and it is inscribed on the scrolls used in the synagogue, consecutive portions of which are read weekly as part of the Sabbath service.

Even before the Scriptures were fully canonized, the historical need arose to reinterpret and apply the Law. Hillel, a Babylonian rabbi by birth, gathered a group of scholars to undertake this task. And the undertaking begun by Hillel was completed nearly two centuries later by Judah Ha-Nasi

(135–219 C.E.), who edited the Mishna, a work in six parts, subdivided under sixty-three headings or tractates written in Hebrew, the language of the Bible.

The Mishna became the heatedly discussed textbook in the academies of two great centers of Jewish learning, one in Jerusalem and the other in Babylon. For several centuries teachers examined the laws as given in the Mishna, commenting on them, interpreting them, and often illuminating their comments and interpretations with parables and legends, or summing up a given principle in a proverb or saying. And many of their discursive lectures were recorded by devoted disciples.

At the time these studies of the Mishna went on in the academies of Jerusalem and Babylon, the Jews did not speak Hebrew but Aramaic, and the recorded discussions, known as Gemara (Completion, or "that which has been learned"), are therefore in Aramaic. The Gemara, together with those portions of the Mishna that were expounded, is called Talmud Torah, or the "Study of the Law," traditionally shortened to Talmud.

There are two versions of the Talmud. One, completed toward the end of the fourth century, resulted from work done in the academy of Jerusalem, the Palestinian Talmud; and the other was the result of the work done in the Babylonian academies, completed in 499 C.E. and known as the Babylonian Talmud. Neither covers all the topics of the Mishna. The Palestinian Talmud covers thirty-nine topics or tractates; and the Babylonian Talmud, thirty-seven. There is reason to believe that all the topics in the Mishna were covered, but some were irrevocably lost. But the Babylonian opus is much more voluminous than the Palestinian, and found greater favor among the people.

The influence of the Babylonian Talmud upon the Jewish people can hardly be overstated. It left its mark on their religious principles and their everyday habits, on their mode of expression and even their pattern of thinking. The historian Heinrich Graetz wrote:

The Babylonian Talmud is especially distinguished by the flights of thought, the penetration of mind, the flashes of genius, which rise and vanish again. . . . The Talmud introduces us into the laboratory of thought, and in it may be traced the progress of ideas, from their earlier agitation to the giddy height of incomprehensibility. . . . It was a family history for succeeding generations, in which they felt themselves at home, in which they lived and moved. . . . For more than a thousand years the external world, nature and mankind, powers and events, were for the Jewish nation insignificant, non-essential, a mere phantom; the only true reality was the Talmud. . . . It created that dialectic, close-reasoning, Jewish spirit, which in the darkest days preserved the dispersed nation from stagnation and stupidity. . . . In a word, the Talmud was the educator of the Jewish nation; and this education can by no means have been a bad one, since, in spite of the disturbing influence of isolation, degradation and systematic demoralization, it fostered in the Jewish people a degree of morality which even their enemies cannot deny them.*

In addition to the Talmud, there are a number of other commentaries on the Bible, known as Midrash. While the Talmud reorganizes, develops, and digests the biblical laws in a topical arrangement, the explanations and expositions, parables and stories of the Midrash follow the biblical text as a running commentary. The most important of these, and the most comprehensive, is "the Great Midrash," devoted to the Five Books of Moses and five other books of the Bible (Song of Songs, Ruth, Lamentations, Ecclesiastes, and Esther), which are associated with five Jewish holidays.

Throughout the Middle Ages commentaries were written for the purpose of clarifying the Bible or the Talmud. Outstanding among the great medieval commentators are Rashi

---

* Heinrich Graetz, *History of the Jews* (Philadelphia, The Jewish Publication Society of America, 1893), II, 634-35.

and Rambam. Rashi (an abbreviation for *R*abbi *Sh*'lomo ben *I*saac) was born in Troyes, France, in 1040 and died there in 1105. He wrote concise, popular commentaries on the entire Babylonian Talmud and on the entire Bible. He opened the door to an understanding of these books for Jews and non-Jews alike.

Rambam (an abbreviation for *R*abbi *M*oses *b*en *M*aimon) is better known as Maimonides. He was born in Cordova, Spain, in 1135 and died in Fostat, Egypt, in 1204. Maimonides was a universal scholar—physician, rabbi, philosopher, linguist, codifier. In his *Guide of the Perplexed* he stirred the Jewish community by expressing the ideals of Judaism in terms of Aristotelian philosophy. He left a lasting imprint in the field of Jewish law with his *Mishne Torah* (*Repetition of the Law*), a clear and systematic codification of talmudic legislation.

It was left to a later writer, however, to produce the definitive Code of Law for the Jews. He was Joseph Caro, who was born in Spain in 1488, and died in Safed, Palestine, in 1575. Caro, outstanding Talmudic scholar of the sixteenth century, spent thirty-five years of his life on the preparation of a gigantic compendium of Jewish Law. He called it *Bet Yosef* (*Joseph's House*), for this was to be a lasting monument to his labors. Almost as an afterthought, he prepared an abridgment of his masterpiece, omitting those laws which had lost their practicality with the destruction of the Temple, omitting details of legal argument, source documentation, historic and geographic variances of practice. He called this four-volume summary *Shulhan Aruk* (*Prepared Table*), for anyone might help himself to the decision of a problem in religious law as he would help himself to food from a table set for a meal.

Joseph Caro was surprised by the success of what he considered his minor effort. Within a few years of its publication, in 1565, edition after edition was sold out. He was equally surprised by the caustic criticism of his contemporaries. "It is suitable only for children and laymen," scorned one scholar. "It is inaccurate," claimed another, "compiled by Caro's students, not himself." The loudest dissent came from the Jews of Germany and Poland, for Caro had reported mainly the practices of the Jews of Spain and the Mediterranean area, the Sephardim. He had disregarded the practices of the Central and East European Jews, the Ashkenazim. One of his most ardent opponents, Rabbi Moses Isserles, took pains to list, in a series of glosses, the thousands of details where the practice of the Jews of Germany and Poland differed from the decisions of the *Shulhan Aruk*. And a surprising thing happened. Isserles' comment did not destroy people's confidence in the *Shulhan Aruk*. On the contrary, they printed Caro's code together with Isserles' glossary; and thus it became the authoritative guide for the Jews in East and West. For orthodox Jews it still is the final authority on most everyday issues of religious law.

Toward the middle of the thirteenth century, long before Caro's work existed, a book of mysticism appeared which was destined to have a profound and lasting influence on large numbers of Jews. The book, by a Spanish Jew, Moses Shem-Tov de Leon, was called *Sepher Ha' Zohar al Ha-Torah* (*The Book of Splendor on the Torah*), and it gave impetus to a movement known as Cabbalah.

The origin of the *Zohar* itself is shrouded in mystery; for De Leon disclaimed authorship of the book and attributed it to Rabbi Simeon ben Yohai, who lived eleven centuries earlier.

The *Zohar*, in part, is a lofty commentary on the Bible. But it also states the Torah can be understood fully only by those who know how to convert its key words into cryptograms and then find their proper, if mystic, interpretation. One must also know the symbolism hidden in the words of

the Bible when the letters of the words are, first, converted
to their numerical value (since each letter in the Hebrew alphabet also represents a numeral) and then replaced by
other words which have the same numerical value. There is
still another system, called permutation, in which certain
letters in words are replaced by the letters in the alphabet
which precede or follow. These create new words, which
presumably reveal the hidden meaning of certain passages.

The significance of the *Zohar* to us, in addition to its value
as a commentary on the Bible, lies in its having inspired a
movement which flourished in the Jewish communities in
Eastern Europe during trying decades and enriched them
with a literature and tradition that has cultural values beyond its Cabbalistic mysticism. This movement, known as
Hasidism, rebelled against the excessive, stern formalism of
legalistic orthodoxy. It emphasized personal piety and close-
ness to God. Hasidism means, literally, "Pietism." Its followers are called Hasidim, "the pious ones."

Of all the books in Jewry's long literary history, the one
which exerted the broadest influence is the Prayerbook.
It reaches back to the time of the Bible. It had its beginnings
in the pages of the Book of Psalms and grew through the
centuries, expressing the hopes and ideals, the suffering and
the gratitude of Jews in every land. It served as the practical
teacher of Jewish thought and ritual to millions who knew
no other textbook. Jewish homes might be without a copy
of the *Shulhan Aruk*, or the Talmud or even the Bible. But
there always was a *Siddur*, a Prayerbook for Sabbaths and
weekdays, and a *Mahzor*, a Prayerbook for the holidays.

The most universal of all Jewish books, the Prayerbook
also reveals accurately historical, local, and ideological differences in the Jewish community. Prayerbooks published
in pre-Hitler Germany bear witness to minute ritual differences between the Jewish communities of Frankfort and
Mainz, a scarce fifty miles apart.

One of the most incisive differences evident in the Prayer-book is that between Spanish and Portuguese Jews, the Sephardim, on the one hand, and the German and East European Jews, the Ashkenazim, on the other. While all Jews scattered over the Roman Empire after the destruction of the Temple, in 70 c.e., based their ritual on the practice of the early synagogue in Palestine and Babylon, the Jews of the Iberian Peninsula were fairly isolated from the Jews of the remainder of Europe from the eighth century until their expulsion in 1492. Each geographic group added to the basic pattern of the ritual prayers expressing its own ideas, its own experience, and its own literary taste. Each group composed different chants and melodies for synagogue use. The very pronunciation of several Hebrew vowels and con-sonants changed under the influence of the environmental languages. To the novice the Hebrew of a Sephardic syna-gogue in New York may sound like an entirely different lan-guage from that of an Ashkenazic house of worship a few blocks distant. The Sephardic pronunciation of Hebrew is accepted in Israel and is therefore becoming increasingly popular among Jews in other countries.

Prayerbooks reveal another interesting historic difference. Editions published by East European Jews, either in Amer-ica or abroad, often have instructions, comments, or trans-lations printed in Hebrew letters but in the Yiddish language—the idiom of East European Jewry, based on the German of the thirteenth century and influenced by Hebrew and the Slavic tongues. Similar instructions, comments, or translations in Hebrew letters may be found in Sephardic editions; but they are in Ladino, a language developed from fifteenth-century Castilian Spanish and used to this day by the descendants of Jews expelled from Spain in the year Columbus discovered America.

The most radical differences among Jewish Prayerbooks published in the United States are those due to the ideological divergence between Orthodoxy, Conservatism, and Reform.

MOVEMENTS IN MODERN JUDAISM

All Jews who identify themselves with their people, in essence, accept their heritage and attempt to preserve it for succeeding generations. All accept the Bible as the foundation of their religion and the record of their early history; and second only to the Bible they value the basic interpretations given in the Talmud, the Midrash, and the added commentaries and codifications which have accrued in the course of centuries and which continue to accrue. All observe the same holidays, most of which are prescribed in the Scriptures; and they value highly the community activities centered in the synagogue.

In their approach, however, to the Bible and its interpretations, in their observance of holidays, and in the liturgical ritual they differ greatly; and their differences have resulted in three distinct movements of Judaism: Orthodox, Conservative, and Reform.

The Orthodox Movement

A leader of Orthodox Jewry in the United States, Rabbi Leo Jung, states the position of the Orthodox group:

Our people never knew any distinctions between Jew and Jew, just as the problems of abstract "theology" did not trouble a true Hebrew, because he satisfied himself with living a life in God. The nineteenth century brought about a change. . . . "Orthos" in Greek means "right" and "doxa" means "opinion." When a part of our brethren broke with the Jewish past and called themselves "reformers" they named those who remained loyal, "orthodox." And for want of a better word in English we may use it to designate the genuine Jew, the man or woman who lives in accordance with Jewish law.*

---

* Rabbi Leo Jung, *Essentials of Judaism* (The Union of Orthodox Jewish Congregations of America).

The Orthodox Jew regards his faith in the Divine origin of the Bible as unchanging and unchangeable, and any deviation a mark of disloyalty. He will allow change in religious matters only if the change conforms with the Law or can be sanctioned within the confines of the Law; otherwise he regards it as mere expediency.

To us Jews the Torah is the book of God, revealed to Israel and through Israel to all men [writes Dr. Jung]. We believe implicity in its Divine origin, we accept it as the standard of our life. We obey its commandments. . . . We know why we should love our neighbor. The Torah says he is "as thyself" (Leviticus 19:18). We know that the Sabbath is a great blessing and that if man generally adopted it, the day of the Messiah would be nearer. But we keep the Sabbath because God has commanded it. Modern medical science endorses the hygienic and eugenic value of Jewish life, of scrupulous compliance with dietary and marriage laws. *But we observe these laws because God commanded them.* As Divine laws we know they are helpful in every way; *but we have adopted them not for their helpfulness, but because God has given them.* [Italics ours.]

The Orthodox are bound by the law as given by Moses or deduced from the Mosaic Law. The authority for their daily practices was "codified" in the sixteenth century by Rabbi Joseph Caro in his work, *Shulhan Aruk.* This code, which at first aroused opposition, is now followed by the Orthodox unswervingly. They observe the dietary laws to the letter; the Sabbath is sanctified, and on it they do not work or travel or transact any business or handle money; and some do not even engage in any mundane conversation. In the synagogue the women are separated from the men by a high partition or are provided with seats in a balcony. In the prayers and ceremonial services Hebrew is used primarily, and they consider the Hebrew language as sacred and inseparable from Judaism as a Faith.

Orthodox Jews are Zionists at heart and support the State

of Israel wholeheartedly. But there are some who look with suspicion on political Zionism because it is secular.

One of the fundamental beliefs of the Jews [writes Dr. Jung], and perhaps the secret of his deathless optimism, is the belief in the coming of the Messiah, a great man of the house of David, who will redeem his people.

The Orthodox quote the Bible to support their Messianic hope, and they see in the Promised Land the Jewish future, and the future of mankind, as foretold by the Prophet Micah:

For out of Zion shall go forth instruction, and the word of the Lord of Jerusalem. And He shall judge between many peoples, and shall decide concerning mighty nations afar off; and they shall beat their swords into plowshares, and their spears into pruning hooks. Nation shall not lift up sword against nation, neither shall they learn war any more. But they shall sit every man under his vine and under his fig-tree, and none shall make them afraid: for the mouth of the Lord of hosts has spoken it. . . . "In that day," says the Lord, "I will assemble her lame, and gather her outcasts and her afflicted, and I will make them into a strong nation. And the Lord shall reign over them in Mount Zion from henceforth and forevermore."

The Conservative Movement

Chronologically, Conservative Judaism appeared about a century after the Reform movement came into being. The Conservative movement in Judaism, as its followers justifiably call it, began in Germany toward the middle of the nineteenth century. But it did not flourish until its transplantation to the United States early in the twentieth century. Dr. Solomon Schechter, then president of the Jewish Theological Seminary, devoted himself to training young rabbis in the Conservative school, "removed alike from both extremes, Radical-Reform and Hyper-Orthodoxy."

As extensions of Dr. Schechter's vision, between 1913 and

1930 there were established the United Synagogue of America, the auxiliary Women's League, the Rabbinical Assembly, the Young People's League, the National Federation of Jewish Men's Clubs—and the Conservative movement began to take roots in Jewish communities throughout the United States.

Those who feel uncomfortable without identifying labels on things or institutions quickly labeled the Conservative movement in Judaism as "the middle of the road between Orthodoxy and Reform." There is only one thing wrong with this description: it isn't entirely accurate. When we examine the movement closely, we find that in some respects it comes very close to Reform in the adoption of certain practices and its basic beliefs, while in most other practices it is difficult to distinguish between the Conservatives and the Orthodox.

The adherents of this movement, according to Dr. Simon Greenberg, Vice-Chancellor of the Jewish Theological Seminary, accept the Jewish heritage essentially as is and find it as relevant and significant today as it ever was, but they

recognize the need for restatement here, refurbishing there, for some subtractions and additions—or, to change the metaphor, for some pruning and grafting. But they believe that the roots, the trunk, and all the main branches are sound, full of sap, capable of and actually producing pleasant fruit.*

Like the Orthodox, the Conservatives accept the Torah; but, unlike the Orthodox, they do not necessarily accept it as of Divine origin.

Our attitude toward our heritage is one of prejudice in its favor [writes Dr. Greenberg]. Our fundamental assumption is that the Torah contains the fullest and sublimest expression of the goals of the holy life that has ever been granted to man and

---

* Simon Greenberg, *The Conservative Movement in Judaism* (The United Synagogue of America).

that the institutions and practices of Judaism, as they developed across the ages, embody the ideals of the Torah. The Ten Commandments, the dietary laws, the injunction to love the stranger as oneself, to honor father and mother, and to observe the festivals need no justification.

The Conservatives recognize the need for constant modifications and adjustments to changing times, to the advance of science and historic circumstances. Judaism, Dr. Greenberg makes clear, has never been a static religion.

We recognize that there were occasions when the challenger of some aspect of the Jewish heritage succeeded in proving his point. Nor do we assume that the heritage will remain unmodified in the future as advancing science, philosophy, and unpredictable historic circumstances make their inexorable claims. But in the future, as in the past, the continuity of Judaism will be triumphantly maintained only by those who, while having open minds, will yet refuse to reform and reconstruct Judaism in accordance with the latest scientific hypotheses, the current popular philosophic fad, or the exigencies of a transient historic circumstance. They have always demanded that the challenger prove his point beyond reasonable doubt—before incorporating the new into the treasure trove of the Jewish heritage.

We do not seek to differentiate ourselves from others [continues Dr. Greenberg]. We gladly accept from others whatever appears to us to make Judaism more meaningful and attractive. We are not afraid of being called Reformed Jews because we accepted the practice, first characteristic of this group, to confirm girls and boys, nor are we afraid of being called Orthodox because we observe the Sabbath traditionally, nor secularists because we believe in the existence of a politically independent Israel. We know that each one of these and many similar practices and ideals help to strengthen Judaism and to make it more meaningful to its followers.

The basic position of the Conservative movement is given in the Preamble to the Constitution of the United Synagogue of America:

The advancement of the cause of Judaism in America and the maintenance of Jewish tradition in its historic continuity; to assert and establish loyalty to the Torah in its historic exposition; to further the observance of the Sabbath and the Dietary Laws; to preserve in the service the reference to Israel's past and the hopes for Israel's restoration; to maintain the traditional character of the liturgy, with Hebrew as the language of prayer; to foster Jewish religious life in the home as expressed in traditional observances; to encourage the establishment of Jewish religious schools, in the curricula of which the study of the Hebrew language and literature shall be given a prominent place, both as the key to the true understanding of Judaism and as a bond holding scattered communities of Israel throughout the world. It shall be the aim of the United Synagogue of America, while not endorsing the innovations introduced by any of its constituent bodies, to embrace all elements essentially loyal to traditional Judaism and in sympathy with the purposes outlined above.

The adherents of the Conservative movement, this statement makes clear, accept the traditional patterns of Judaism. But they have also instituted, to use Dr. Greenberg's metaphor, "some pruning and grafting" in their practice, although the pruning and grafting are not imposed uniformly on all adherents. For their authority in allowing "innovation without regimentation" they quote the Mishna: "In communities where it was the custom not to work on the eve of Passover, it was not permissible to work; and in those communities where it was the custom to work on the eve of the Passover, it was permissible to work."

With these basic concepts to guide them, the Conservative movement in Judaism approaches the task of preserving and strengthening Jewish life.

The Reform Movement

The Reform movement in Judaism claims that for centuries the dominant concept of Judaism has been that the conduct of the individual, as well as the community, was

determined and regulated by Law. At no time could a Jew
be a law unto himself. There was a "thou shalt" and a "thou
shalt not" for every conceivable occasion—all emanating
from an interpretation of the basic commandments and precepts as given in the Torah, repeated in the Mishna, and
interpreted in the Midrash or the Talmud. But the application of each of the precepts has been subjected to diverse,
often conflicting, interpretations; and what was accepted
and practiced in one place and time became permissible in
that place and time, even though it was inconsistent with
the practice of other communities. All precepts emanated
from a basic core of faith, but their application was always
subject to interpretation and dependent on historic circumstances.

This acceptance of Judaism as a dynamic and ever-adjust-
ing way of life rather than a static creed resulted in great
controversies in talmudic times; and controversies arose
throughout the centuries.

But when the Jews were subjected to unprecedented per-
secutions from the fifteenth to the eighteenth centuries, and
restricted to ghettos, they responded by building a fence
around tradition. They again codified their rules of behavior
in the *Shulhan Aruk* and attempted to formulate a rigid
and immutable cast for all adherents.

With the period of enlightenment that came in the
eighteenth century, when the Jews in Germany came out of
the ghettos and began to participate in the general cultural
life of their communities, there arose among them a movement designed to loose Judaism from its rigid cast so that
it could be free, as in the past, to adapt itself to the new
times. This movement was called "Reform." The reformers
of Judaism wished to remain within the fold of their ancient
Faith, but wanted to subject its beliefs and practices to the
test of contemporary needs.

A leader of the Reform movement in Judaism, Rabbi Abraham J. Feldman, writes:

Reform is classical Judaism asserting anew the right and the duty of accelerating the process of progress and change where changes seem to be necessary. If some customs and practices are no longer meaningful, then they are no longer useful, and to cling to them mechanically or to acknowledge them as valid whilst they are largely neglected is to endanger the very survival of Jews and Judaism. . . . Therefore, Reform's principal contribution is the decision to keep Judaism forever contemporary, and to keep it responsive to the religious needs of successive generations. Its purpose is not to preserve, let us say, in Hartford, or in Brooklyn, or in Chicago, or even in the United States of America, all the forms of the Judaism of Poland, of Galicia, Hungary, Rumania, or Lithuania, but to keep Judaism Jewish in content whilst adapting the traditional forms to contemporary life, and creating new forms as needs require. . . . Reform insists that changes be made *when* they are needed, *in* and *by* the generation that needs them, rather than wait generations or even centuries before any perceptible adjustments occur. Our generations today and the generations tomorrow have the right and, we think, the duty to keep Judaism alive by keeping it contemporary, and responsive to their spiritual needs.*

Like the Conservative movement, the Reform movement was brought from Germany to this country, where it fluorished. Its organizing genius was Rabbi Isaac Mayer Wise, who came here toward the middle of the nineteenth century and established the Union of American Hebrew Congregations. Soon afterward he founded the Hebrew Union College, which had as its objective the training of rabbis as deeply aware of American culture and American life as they were of the discipline of classical Judaism. During the next few decades the Reform movement slowly clarified and organized an approach to Judaism more consistent with con-

---

* Rabbi Abraham J. Feldman, *Reform Judaism* (Behrman House, New York).

temporary American life. Women are not segregated in any of the religious services. Musical instruments are used to enrich the services. The custom of covering the head with a hat or skullcap during services, a custom common in the Orient, where it denotes respect, has been abandoned. The use of the prayer shawl and phylacteries (*t'filin*) has been discontinued. The dietary laws are not mandatory. And other changes have been instituted.

Some innovations introduced by the Reform have since been adopted by the Conservative, and some even by the Orthodox. They have led the way in techniques of congregational organization. Late Friday evening services, introduced by Reform, were adopted by all Conservative and some Orthodox synagogues. Confirmation of boys and girls in their fifteenth or sixteenth year, adopted by the German reformers in 1810, has been accepted by all Conservative synagogues in this country, and by many Orthodox. Though at first the Reform were vehemently attacked for allowing men and women to sit together during services, the practice was later adopted by the Conservatives. The modification of the Prayerbook, first introduced by Reform, led to the modification of the Conservative Prayerbook.

In time, however, Reform reintroduced and reinterpreted some of the traditional customs which early radical reformers had eliminated. And so each movement made its independent contribution to the revitalization of Judaism today.

Reconstructionism

Added to the three main movements of Judaism in America which had their origin in other lands, there is an indigenous movement of great promise, Reconstructionism, which was founded in the 1930's by Dr. Mordecai M. Kaplan.

The objectives of Reconstructionism are to revitalize the

Jewish religion and to enrich the Jewish tradition so that Jews in a modern democratic society can give greater meaning to their lives while contributing to the cultural life of the general community. The objectives are based on the belief that Judaism can be reinterpreted to meet the intellectual demands and spiritual needs of life in contemporary America.

Reconstructionism views Judaism as a dynamic religious civilization, which, in America, must be lived simultaneously with the primary civilization of our land. To live in two civilizations at the same time, Jews need to make the following adjustments in their Judaism: (1) To restore the spiritual unity of the Jewish people; (2) to continue to aid in the development of Israel; (3) to create an organic, democratic structure for Jewish communal life; (4) to revitalize Jewish religion; (5) to encourage Jewish cultural creativity in education, literature and the arts; (6) to intensify participation by Jews in all activities furthering the ideals of American democracy.*

Dr. Kaplan establishes the following as the Principles of Reconstructionism:

1. Judaism, or that which has united the successive generations of Jews into one People, is not only a religion; it is a dynamic religious civilization.
2. Judaism has passed through three distinct stages in its evolution, and is now on the threshold of a fourth stage. It was national during the First Commonwealth era, ecclesiastic during the Second Commonwealth era, and rabbinic from then until the end of the eighteenth century. It is now developing into a democratic civilization.
3. The emergence of the next stage calls for the reconstruction of the Jewish People and its enhancement, the revitalization of Jewish religion, and the replenishment of Jewish culture.
4. The reconstitution of the Jewish People is predicated upon the following:

---

* *A Way of Life for the Modern Jew* (Reconstructionist Press).

    a. the reclamation of the Land of Israel as the home of the historic Jewish civilization;

    b. the renewal of the covenant binding all Jews throughout the world into one united People, with the Jewish community in Israel as the core;

    c. the formation of organic Jewish communities in all countries of the Jewish Diaspora.

5. An organic community is one in which all activities and institutions conducted by Jews for Jews are interactive, and in which the fostering of Jewish peoplehood, religion, and culture is given primacy.

6. The revitalization of religion can be best achieved through the study of it in the spirit of free inquiry and through the separation of church and state.

7. The revitalization of the Jewish religion required that the belief in God be interpreted in terms of universally human, and of specifically Jewish experience.

8. By reason of the diversity in world outlook, there has to be room in Jewish religion for different versions of it.

9. The continuity of a religion through different stages, and its identity amid diversity of belief and practice, are sustained by its sancta: these are the heroes, events, texts, places, and seasons that the religion signalizes as furthering the fulfillment of human destiny.

10. The traditional conception of Torah should be expanded to mean:

    a. ethical culture, the fostering of love and justice in all human relations;

    b. ritual culture, the fostering of the religious sancta with all of their symbolic significance;

    c. esthetic culture, the fostering of the arts as a means of expressing the emotional values of Jewish life.

11. Every People, Jewish or non-Jewish, is nowadays confronted with the problem of living in two civilizations. It has to blend its historic civilization with the modern civilization of the country in which it lives.

12. Loyalty to Judaism should be measured by active participation in Jewish life, in keeping with the foregoing principles.

Reconstructionism is not an independent and separate movement, but one that strives to find disciples and followers in the entire Jewish community, Orthodox, Conservative, or Reform, and to help all Jews "to meet the unprecedented challenge of our age."

REVIVAL OF JUDAISM IN AMERICA

Preoccupation with the revitalization of Judaism for America is significant particularly as a response to a historic necessity.

In the Western world during the nineteenth and early part of the twentieth centuries, religion in general suffered a decline. Allegiance was transferred to science in the belief that it could solve all mankind's problems and answer all life's puzzling questions. But the two world wars, coming in quick succession, brought about a great disillusionment. Man was faced with the stark realization that he had at last perfected a means to destroy himself, but was as far as ever from the Golden Age promised by the prophets of all the great religions. Science had failed to satisfy man's spiritual needs, and offered no answers to the questions uppermost in his mind; and there was a gradual and increasing return to religion.

The increased religious awareness among American Jews had several additional incentives. In a single decade, over a third of all the Jews in the world had been brutally annihilated simply because they were Jews. And in another decade the State of Israel was almost miraculously created, where some of the persecuted remnant found refuge. These two events, one of great sorrow and the other of great rejoicing, shocked American Jews into an unprecedented awareness of themselves, for now the majority of Jews in the world lived in America. In the infant State of Israel, which American Jews understandably supported to the limit of their ability, the Israeli Jews were building their own civilization. In America the American Jews wished to orient their lives so as to integrate their American nationality with their heritage of Judaism. And this gave rise to modifications, reinterpretations, and re-evaluations of Judaism in America.

The most important effect has been the general resurgence of Judaism in all its branches or movements, and the earnestness with which its adherents search for spiritual solace in an age of doubt and confusion. As never before in their history, American Jews are re-examining their heritage and trying to learn what it means to be a Jew.

THE JEWISH ATTITUDE TOWARD ISRAEL

In Judaism the Promised Land occupies a prominent place as the soil upon which the spiritual and cultural growth of Israel was predestined to flourish. The concept goes back to the day, as told in the Bible, when God said to Abraham:

Depart from your country and from your kindred, and go to the land that I will show you. And I will make of you a great nation, and bless you, and make your name great. I will bless him who blesses you, and curse him who curses you, and in you shall the families of the earth be blessed (Genesis 12:1-3).

Thus, by Divine Covenant, the Promised Land was given as an inheritance to the descendants of Abraham, Isaac, and Jacob, a land upon which they were to fulfill their mission of bringing the Divine Law to mankind.

Later, many centuries later, when the kingdoms of Israel and Judah were destroyed and their inhabitants scattered to the four corners of the earth, they took with them into the dispersion the Messianic hope developed by the prophets and linked with the original concept of the Promised Land. Throughout the long and trying centuries the Jews never abandoned this sustaining hope. In times of black despair their souls were revived and their courage uplifted as they reassured themselves:

Behold, the days come, saith the Lord, that the plowman shall overtake the reaper, and the treader of grapes him that soweth the seed; and the mountains shall drop sweet wine, and all the hills shall melt. And I will turn the captivity of My people Israel, and they shall build the waste cities, and inhabit them; and they shall plant the vineyards, and drink the wine thereof; they shall also make gardens, and eat the fruit of them. And I will plant them upon their land, and they shall no more be plucked up out of their land which I have given them, saith the Lord my God (Amos 9:13-15).

From time to time there would arise a man who claimed to be the hoped-for Redeemer of the Children of Israel, and fortified his claim with scriptural citations. These men appeared in Persia, in Palestine, in France, in Spain, and in other countries where the Jews dwelt. The most noted of these pseudo-Messiahs was Sabbatai Zevi (1626–76), who, at the age of twenty-two, proclaimed himself the Messiah foretold by the prophets; and he designated the year 1666 as the year of the millennium. The hope among the faithful rose high, and great was their rejoicing. When the year 1666 arrived and Sabbatai Zevi, to save himself from death, embraced Islam, their joy turned into sorrow. But though their bright hope for the Restoration of Zion was dimmed in times of disillusion, it was never extinguished.

During the Puritan revolution in England and in other European countries, the Restoration of Zion found an increasing number of zealous supporters among Christian leaders, who saw in it the prerequisite condition for their own hoped-for Second Coming of Christ. Many plans were evolved by them, particularly in England and France, to restore the Jews to their homeland and to help them reestablish themselves as a spiritual and cultural community. The advocacy of Zionism among the Christians constitutes a conspicuous and romantic chapter in European history. In the nineteenth century particularly we find almost all the great humanitarians among the preachers and teachers, the poets and novelists, the reformers and social thinkers, at one time or another concerned with the Restoration of Zion.

Then, toward the end of the nineteenth century, modern Zionism came into existence with the publication, in 1897, of *The Jewish State* by Theodor Herzl. On the title page of this pamphlet Dr. Herzl wrote: *"If you will it, it need not remain a dream."* He foretold that if the Jews "will it" the State of Israel could be realized within fifty years. And almost exactly fifty years later, on May 14, 1948, David Ben-Gurion, leader in Israel, arose in the Art Museum of Tel Aviv to proclaim the establishment of the Jewish State; and Israel once again took its place as a nation among the nations.

Excepting for only a few of the extremely Orthodox and the advocates of total assimilation, the State of Israel has attracted the devoted support of Jews throughout the world. They see how Israel, at the very moment of its birth, became the refuge for survivors of the German extermination camps to whom all other avenues of escape were closed. They recognize it as a home for the homeless, a haven "by right and not by suffrance" for victims of oppression. They also look to Israel as a cultural center. They remember with admiration the literary and artistic productivity of the pioneers even while they were building and defending their new state, literally, with a plow in one hand and a gun in the other. They expect a growth and a deepening of Jewish values from an active interchange in the fields of art and music, literature and religion between Israel and the Jews of America and other countries. They believe that Israel will speed among all Jews a spiritual awakening in which the tradition of the past will be linked with the future, and in its light "shall all the families of the earth be blessed."

PART II

THE DAILY PRAYERS*

"O Lord, open Thou my lips,
and my mouth shall declare Thy praise."
—Psalms 51:17

---

* All prayers quoted in this section come from *The Authorized Daily Prayerbook* by Joseph H. Hertz, symbolized by *O-1;* and *The Union Prayerbook for Jewish Worship,* symbolized by *R-1.*

HOW PRAYER GREW

SINCE TIME IMMEMORIAL prayer has been at the very core of Jewish life. For a people who were always conscious of God's presence, prayer was an ever-available means of communication.

When Abraham learned that God was about to destroy the wicked cities of Sodom and Gomorrah, he was deeply concerned. Was God going to destroy everyone, innocent and guilty alike? Was God acting justly? Or was this an act of angry retribution? So Abraham prayed. He poured his concern and his doubts into words of prayer.

Prayer might be the outcry of the Pharaoh's slave as he bent his back under the lash. Prayer might be the soldier's shout of victory over the crumbling walls of Jericho. Prayer might be a people's plea for water in a parched wilderness. Prayer might be a mother's whispered "I thank Thee," at the birth of her child. Prayer might be the affirmation of faith in God's unity.

Communication with God was not always through the spoken word. Nor was prayer the main form of worship in the early days of our religion. On most special occasions people would worship God by means of sacrifice.

When Cain and Abel wanted to express their thanks to God, "Cain brought to the Lord an offering of the fruit of the ground, and Abel brought of the firstlings of his flock" (Genesis 5:3-4).

When Abraham entered into solemn covenant with God, receiving assurance that his descendants would be as numer-

ous as the stars and would possess the Promised Land, he
brought an offering of "a heifer three years old, a she-goat
three years old, a ram three years old, a turtledove, and a
young pigeon" (Genesis 15:9). Abraham even showed himself willing to sacrifice his son Isaac; for child sacrifice,
though always condemned by Judaism, was an accepted form
of worship among the non-Hebrew people of Abraham's
time and for two thousand years after his time.

A major portion of the books of Leviticus and Numbers
is devoted to a detailed description of the sacrifices that were
to be brought to God on various occasions, on Passover,
Pentecost, and the Festival of Booths, on the New Year and
the Day of Atonement, on the Sabbath, on the New Moon,
and on the ordinary weekday. There were offerings after the
birth of a child and after recovery from illness. There were
guilt offerings and sacrifices of thanksgiving. There were offerings of heifers and lambs and doves, of flour, of oil, and
of wine.

These sacrifices were never offered in complete silence.
The priests would chant as they performed their sacred
tasks. On the Day of Atonement, for instance, the sixteenth
chapter of Leviticus bids the high priest make confession
of "all the iniquities of the people of Israel," as he prepares
the scapegoat for sacrifice. The Mishna records the high
priest's prayer on this occasion:

O God, Thy people, the house of Israel, have sinned, they have
committed iniquity, they have transgressed against Thee; I beseech Thee by Thy Name, make Thou atonement for the sins
and for the iniquities and for the transgressions, wherein Thy
people, the house of Israel, have sinned and committed iniquity
and transgressed against Thee; as it is written in the Law of Thy
servant Moses at Thy command, "For on this day shall atonement be made for you, to cleanse you: from all your sins before
the Lord shall you be clean."

And the priests and the people who were in the Temple would kneel down, prostrate themselves, and respond: "Praised be His name Whose glorious kingdom is forever and ever" (Mishna Yoma 6:2).

While a formal liturgy began to grow around the sacrificial service at the sanctuary, prayer never was limited to these formal occasions. According to talmudic tradition the three patriarchs started the custom of praying three times each day. Abraham introduced the morning prayer; Isaac, the afternoon service; and Jacob, the evening devotions.

Moses prayed on many occasions. In the hour of triumph on the Red Sea he sang with his people: "Who is like Thee, O Lord, among the mighty? Who is like Thee, majestic in holiness, terrible in glorious deeds, doing wonders?" (Exodus 15:11). When God condemned the people for their worship of the golden calf, Moses entreated Him:

O Lord, why does Thy wrath burn hot against Thy people whom Thou hast brought forth out of the land of Egypt with great power and with a mighty hand? . . . Turn from Thy fierce wrath. Remember Abraham, Isaac, and Israel, Thy servants to whom Thou didst swear by Thine own self, and didst say to them, "I will multiply your descendants as the stars of heaven, and all this land that I have promised I will give to your descendants, and they shall inherit it forever" (Exodus 32:11-14).

When he came to the end of his journey, at the banks of the river Jordan, Moses prayed: "O Lord God, let me go over and see the good land beyond the Jordan!" Yet, in his final hour he exclaimed:

> There is none like God, O Jeshurun,
> Who rides through the heavens to your help,
> And in His majesty through the skies. . . .
> Happy are you, O Israel, . . .
> A people saved by the Lord.
>
> (Deuteronomy 33:26, 29)

The Bible abounds with examples of personal prayer.

There is the story of Hannah, in the first chapter of I Samuel, who prayed, "O Lord of hosts, if Thou wilt indeed look on the affliction of Thy maidservant, and remember me, and not forget Thy maidservant, but wilt give to Thy maidservant a son, then I will give him to the Lord all the days of his life." She "continued praying . . . speaking in her heart; only her lips moved, and her voice was not heard." And when she was blessed with a son, she prayed again:

> My heart exults in the Lord;
> My strength is exalted in the Lord. . . .
> There is none holy like the Lord,
> There is none besides Thee;
> There is no rock like our God. (I Samuel 2:1-2)

There is Solomon's humble prayer for wisdom:

O Lord my God, Thou hast made Thy servant king in place of David my father, although I am but a little child; I do not know how to go out or come in. . . . Give Thy servant therefore an understanding mind to govern Thy people, that I may discern between good and evil. (I Kings 3:7-9)

And his majestic prayer at the dedication of the Temple:

"Behold, heaven and the highest heaven cannot contain Thee; how much less this house which I have built!" (I Kings, 8:27)

There is Daniel's prayer of confession and entreaty, parts of which are still used in the Atonement liturgy:

We have sinned and done wrong and acted wickedly and rebelled, turning aside from Thy Commandments and ordinances. . . . To Thee, O Lord, belongs righteousness, but to us confusion of face. . . . To the Lord our God belong mercy and forgiveness; but we have rebelled against Him. . . . O Lord, hear; O Lord, forgive; O Lord, give heed and act; delay not, for Thy own sake, O my God, because Thy city and Thy people are called by Thy name. (Daniel 9:5-19)

By far the greatest collection of prayers is found in the Book of Psalms. Tradition ascribes the authorship of most of the one hundred and fifty Psalms of the Bible to King David. In effect, they reflect the thoughts and feelings, the hopes and disappointments, the sufferings and the hostilities of many people over many centuries.

Many of the Psalms probably were written expressly to be sung during the sacrificial service at the sanctuary by the Levite choirs which King David had organized. Like Psalm 95—which still opens the Sabbath eve service in the synagogue—these Psalms are addressed to the worshiper:

> O Come, let us sing unto the Lord;
> Let us shout for joy to the Rock of our salvation.
> Let us come before His presence with thanksgiving,
> Let us shout for joy unto Him with psalms."

Others were sung by the pilgrims from the cities and villages of Israel and the Diaspora as they marched toward Jerusalem to celebrate the Passover, Pentecost, or the Feast of Booths—for instance, Psalm 122:

> I rejoiced when they said unto me:
> "Let us go to the House of the Lord."

Some Psalms are national in scope and resound with the gratitude of a redeemed people, as does Psalm 107:

> O give thanks unto the Lord, for He is good,
> For His mercy endureth forever.
> So let the redeemed of the Lord say,
> Whom He hath redeemed from the hand of the adversary;
> And gathered them out of the lands,
> From the east and from the west,
> From the north and from the sea.

Others reflect the anguish of the individual soul, such as Psalm 22:

My God, my God, why hast Thou forsaken me,
And art far from my help at the words of my cry?

Or deepest confidence in God's protection, as Psalm 23:

The Lord is my shepherd, I shall not want.
He maketh me to lie down in green pastures;
He leadeth me beside the still waters.
He restoreth my soul;
He guideth me in straight paths for His name's sake.

Many Psalms express man's admiration for God's universe, as, for instance, Psalm 19:

The heavens declare the glory of God,
And the firmament showeth His handiwork.

Others meditate on the meaning of man's life, such as Psalm 90:

The days of our years are threescore years and ten,
Or even by reason of strength fourscore years;
Yet is their pride but travail and vanity;
For it is speedily gone, and we fly away.

The Book of Psalms contains the song of the warrior—"Blessed be the Lord my Rock, Who traineth my hands for war, and my fingers for battle" (Psalms 144:1)—along with the prayer for peace: "Pray for the peace of Jerusalem; may they prosper that love Thee" (Psalms 122:6); "The Lord will give strength unto His people; The Lord will bless His people with peace" (Psalms 29:11).

A NEW INSTITUTION IS BORN

In the course of the centuries prayer came to be a more and more important part of our people's religious life. This was partly due to the warnings by the prophets against overconfidence in the sacrifices as a way to God's favor:

> With what shall I come before the Lord,
> And bow myself before God on high?
> Shall I come before Him with burnt offerings,
> With calves a year old?
> Will the Lord be pleased with thousands of rams,
> With ten thousands of rivers of oil?
> Shall I give my first-born for my transgression,
> The fruit of my body for the sin of my soul?
> He has showed you, O man, what is good;
> And what does the Lord require of you
> But to do justice, and to love kindness,
> And to walk humbly with your God? (Micah 6:6-8)

The Psalmist proclaimed:

The sacrifices of God are a broken spirit;
A broken and contrite heart, O God, Thou wilt not despise
                    (Psalms 51:19; AV, Psalms 51:17)

And prayer was the voice of the contrite heart.

The importance of prayer also increased with the distance between the dwellings of the Jewish people and the central sanctuary in Jerusalem, where alone sacrifices could be offered. During the first exile, when the Babylonians had destroyed Solomon's Temple, the captives by the rivers of Babylon followed Jeremiah's instruction to "seek the welfare of the city where I have sent you into exile, and pray to the Lord on its behalf" (Jeremiah 29:7).

Even after Ezra and Nehemiah had rebuilt Jerusalem with its magnificent Temple, and offerings were again brought there on behalf of the entire people, Jews still gathered in meeting places throughout the Holy Land as well as in Babylon to recite their prayers. At the very hour the priests, as the representatives of the people, officiated at the Temple, the people themselves brought the offering of their prayers at community halls and school buildings which subsequently came to be known as synagogues.

After the second and final destruction of the Temple under the Romans in 70 C.E., the young institution of the synagogue proved strong enough to take the place of the Temple in the minds of the people. To be sure, the Jews would always remember with deep affection "the great and holy house which was called by Thy name." For two thousand years they would pray for the return to a Jerusalem to be rebuilt "as in times of yore." Meanwhile they reconstructed a complete religion around the synagogue in lieu of the Temple, and prayer effectively and completely replaced the act of sacrifice as a means of communication with God.

A PORTABLE HOMELAND

With the dispersion of the Jews throughout the Roman Empire, danger arose that they would assimilate, and that their religion would dissolve and disappear. This was indeed the aim of Titus when he destroyed the Temple, in 70 C.E., and of Hadrian when he prohibited the teaching and practice of the Jewish religion in Palestine, sixty-eight years later. The Jews were a people without a political homeland. They had a religion without conventional central authority.

Three books, above all else, made possible the survival of Judaism and of the Jews against all odds: the Bible, the Talmud and the Prayerbook. They became to the Jews a central religious authority and a spiritual homeland which they could carry along on their journeys, from country to country. The presence of these volumes—or even of their content in men's memories—could make any home into a house of God, any meeting hall into a synagogue.

The Bible was always the primary influence of Judaism. But of the Talmud and the Prayerbook, the latter exerted a greater influence by far on the average Jew. The Talmud was an entire library in itself. It represented an almost stenographic report of scholarly discussions in the academies of Israel and Babylonia over a period of five hundred years. Its maze of argument and counter argument, of biblical law and postbiblical interpretations was the domain of scholars. And even among a scholarly people those who were really at home in the world of the Talmud were a minority.

The Prayerbook, on the other hand, was the religious guide for the average Jew. It told him when to pray and what prayers to recite on every important occasion. Fortunately, the basic framework of the liturgy had been established by the time of the dispersion. In the Mishna, the earliest stratum of talmudic literature, we find provisions for the recitation every morning and evening of the *Sh'ma*, the affirmation of God's unity, with its introductory and succeeding blessings. The Talmud likewise refers to the collection of eighteen benedictions known as the *T'filah*, "The Prayer," which is recited morning, afternoon, and evening and which is adapted to express the ideas of the Sabbath and the various holidays. The reading of the Law and the Prophets on each Sabbath and holiday as well as on Mondays and Thursdays was likewise fixed at an early date.

The pattern of Jewish worship was clearly discernible by the time Christianity began to develop. The sounds of early synagogue music still re-echo in some of the Gregorian chants of the Roman Catholic and Eastern Orthodox churches. And certain portions of the Mass are similar to portions of the Jewish liturgy.

It is most amazing that the synagogue service remained identical except for minor details in most countries of the Diaspora. Throughout the upheavals caused by the expansion of Christianity, the fall of the Roman Empire, and the subsequent rise of Islam, the Jewish communities of the East and the West maintained sufficient contact to develop the same liturgy. This is how the Prayerbook took final shape. During the second half of the ninth century the Jews of Barcelona, Spain, wanted to make certain that they were reciting the proper prayers in the proper order in their synagogue. They therefore sent an inquiry to the Gaon Amram of Sura, Babylonia, who was considered the greatest Hebrew scholar of the age. In reply Amram carefully set forth the order of prayers for weekdays, for Sabbaths, and for every holiday of the year, based on the record of the Talmud and on the practice of the great Babylonian academies. The Jews of Barcelona found the document most helpful. Subsequently copies of the *Order of Prayer of Rab Amram* circulated through Spain and France and Germany, where it became the standard order of service.

In the centuries that followed, the Jews of Spain and Portugal added poetic portions to the holiday services. The communities of France and Germany, Russia and Poland made different additions. In modern times Prayerbooks were published with translations and commentaries in the language of each country. Still, if anyone enters a synagogue in New York or Buenos Aires, in Paris or Budapest, in Rome or Tel Aviv or Melbourne, he will find the prayers almost identical, the atmosphere of the service very similar.

The most radical changes in the service have been made by the Reform or liberal movement. Since the early part of the nineteenth century, Reform Prayerbooks have been published in German, English, and French. Most of these volumes eliminate the repetitions of the Orthodox service and excise references to the re-establishment of the sacrificial service, the coming of a personal Messiah, and the physical resurrection of the dead. Prayers are printed in Hebrew and translated or paraphrased in the vernacular. In fact, some prayers appear only in the vernacular. Still, the basic order of prayer follows age-old tradition.

WHEN DO WE PRAY?

Jewish tradition provides for three prayer services each day. The morning service (*Shahrit*) should open the new day. The afternoon service (*Minhah*) brings spiritual refreshment in the midst of the busy day. The evening service (*Ma'ariv*) after sunset offers an opportunity to express thanks for the blessings of the day and to pray for a restful night.

In effect, there are additional periods for worship. While the daily evening service is recited before the evening meal, an additional brief service is provided at the time of retiring. The Talmud further encourages the especially pious to rouse themselves at midnight in order to recite Psalms.

On Sabbaths and holidays an additional service (*Musaf*) follows immediately upon the morning prayers, and, on the Day of Atonement, a special service of conclusion (*N'ilah*) is added after the afternoon service.

Jewish tradition has arranged for the recitation of prayers at fixed times; for the habit of regular prayer is a prerequisite of community prayer. Also, it has been said that the Prayerbook will bring inspiration to those who read it at the set time of prayer. But he who waits for inspiration may never get to open his Prayerbook.

In addition to the daily prayers which follow a fixed time schedule, there are many prayers which are entirely independent of time. These are the blessings recited whenever we enjoy any of God's gifts. At every meal, regardless of when it is eaten, we break bread and say: "Praised be Thou, O Lord our God, Ruler of the World, Who bringest bread out of the earth." Grace after meals praises the Lord "Who, in His goodness feeds the whole world, Who gives food to all the living, for His kindness endures forever." In addition to prayers for a livelihood, for God's blessing on the family and the home, and for food for humanity, the grace includes petitions for the redemption of the Jewish people, for freedom of the enslaved, and for universal peace.

There are special blessings to be recited over food to be eaten outside of mealtimes. They praise the "Ruler of the world Who creates the fruit of the tree," ". . . the fruit of the earth," ". . . the fruit of the vine." Any food not included in these classifications is covered by the praising of Him "by Whose word all things exist."

Before eating anything at all, we wash our hands and praise "the Lord our God, Ruler of the world, Who has sanctified us by His laws and commanded us the washing of hands."

There are words of thanks for every enjoyable experience—on smelling fragrant fruits or plants or spices, on seeing blossoming trees or lofty mountains or the rainbow or the sea.

When we hear thunder, we praise Him "Whose strength and might fill the world." On tasting a species of fruit for the first time in the season, on entering a new home, or enjoying a new garment, we thank Him "Who has kept us alive, Who has preserved us and has enabled us to reach this season."

There is even a blessing to be recited on seeing a king and his court. It is said of King George V of England that he noticed a group of elderly Jews along his route every time he traveled through Hyde Park. They watched intently and respectfully as he passed and their mouths seemed to move in an inaudible whisper. He was curious whether they had come all the way from Whitechapel just to see their monarch. So one day he stopped to inquire. One of the Jews enlightened the King: "Our religion bids us praise the Lord at least a hundred times each day. Seeing Your Majesty gives us one more opportunity to recite a blessing."

WHAT DO WE PRAY FOR?

Just as most of the blessings for special occasions take the form of praise and of thanksgiving, so the fixed daily prayers contain many more words of gratitude and adoration than they do words of plaint and petition. The daily morning prayer opens with thanksgiving for a healthy body which comes from Him "Who is the wondrous healer of all flesh"; and for the soul, "Thou hast created it, Thou hast formed it, Thou hast breathed it into me." We thank Him for refreshing sleep and for the miracle of awakening to new life. We thank Him for strength of hand and sight of eye, for shelter and clothing, for freedom and comfort, and for guidance in all things found in His Law.

We approach God in humility: "Lord of all worlds, not in reliance upon our own merit do we lay our supplications before Thee, but trusting in Thine infinite mercy alone. For what are we, what is our life, what our goodness, what our power?" (*O-1*, p. 26, *R-1*, p. 101).

The introductory prayers of the daily morning service are followed by the recitation of Psalms of thanksgiving and of praise, notably Psalms 145 to 150, which are introduced by the verse from Psalm 84: "Happy are they who dwell in Thy house, they are ever praising Thee." Other laudatory passages selected from I Chronicles and Nehemiah, from Exodus and Zechariah, lead up to the majestic call to worship which, in the days of the early synagogue, may have marked the very beginning of the service: "Praise ye the Lord, to Whom all praise is due" (*O-1*, p. 108).

Worship continues with words of praise for "Him Who in His goodness renews daily the work of creation. How manifold are Thy works, O Lord. In wisdom hast Thou made them all." This is followed by the affirmation that God gave His Law as an expression of His love for His people. "Thou hast chosen us from all peoples and tongues.

Thou hast brought us close to Thee that we might thank Thee and proclaim Thy unity" (O-1, p. 116).

To proclaim God's unity is the primary purpose of all Jewish prayer. "Hear O Israel, the Lord our God, the Lord is One." This quotation from Deuteronomy (6:4-9) is here recited solemnly, followed by the commandment to "love the Lord with all thy heart and all thy soul and all thy might." A parallel passage from Deuteronomy (11:13-21) and the commandment concerning fringes on the corners of the garment completes the didactic prayer known as the *Sh'ma*. A prayer of thanks for God's help to our fathers in ages past and for the redemption of our people from Egyptian slavery concludes the first section of the morning service.

The next section is a collection of benedictions which forms the central part of every synagogue service, weekday, Sabbath, or festival; morning, afternoon, "additional," or evening. It is known as "The Eighteen" (*Sh'mone Esre*), for in its original, complete form it consisted of that number of paragraphs each ending with the prayer formula "Praised be Thou, O Lord . . ." Because of its importance in Jewish tradition it is also known as "The Prayer" (*T'filah*), or as "The Standing Prayer" (*Amidah*), because it is to be recited while standing.

This collection is a perfect illustration of the Jewish philosophy of worship. It begins with three blessings of praise which are identical in all services. God is adored as the "shield of Abraham," as the Almighty God, Creator of all, Who "remembers the devotion of the fathers and brings redemption to the children." He is glorified as "Support of the falling, Healer of the sick and Deliverer of the captives" . . . "Who revives the dead," or, in the Reform version, "Who has implanted within us eternal life."

The third of these opening benedictions is the "Sanctification" (*K'dushah*). In congregational worship its responses represent a musical climax of the service. Composers have written many different melodies for this passage; and the exact wording of the paragraph differs from weekday to Sabbath and festival, from morning to "additional" service, from Spanish to German to East European tradition, from Orthodox to Reform interpretation. But all of them are paraphrases of the identical theme. They are the attempt to express in word and music the idea of God's holiness, which is beyond the power of man's understanding, let alone of man's language.

All versions of the Sanctification are based on three quotations from Scripture: "Holy, holy, holy is the Lord of Hosts, the whole earth is full of His glory" (Isaiah 6:3); the puzzling "Praised be the Glory of the Lord from His place" (Ezekiel 3:12), and "The Lord shall reign forever, thy God, O Zion, from generation to generation, Halleluyah" (Psalms: 146:10).

The central group of benedictions is known as "Petitions." Even these, however, ask God's gifts for the entire world or for all Jews rather than for the individual. They, too, usually open with a statement of man's indebtedness to God rather than a request. The form of the first petition is characteristic for the group: "Thou favourest man with knowledge, and teachest mortals understanding. O favour us with knowledge, understanding, and discernment from Thee. Blessed art Thou, O Lord, gracious Giver of knowledge" (O-1, pp. 136-38).

Subsequent paragraphs ask for God's help in repentance, for His forgiveness of our sins, for His salvation in affliction, for His healing of the sick, for His blessing upon the fields. They plead for redemption and gathering-in of the exiles, for the establishment of God's kingdom, for the destruction of wickedness, for the reward of the righteous, for the rebuilding of Jerusalem, and for the coming of the Messiah. A petition that "God may hear our voice and accept our prayer in mercy" concludes this group of petitions.

In the earliest version of The Prayer there were twelve paragraphs in this middle group. Together with the three opening and three closing benedictions, they added up to eighteen. During the period of persecution by the Romans, when the Jews were plagued by informers who denounced to the authorities those who secretly practiced their ancestral Faith, an additional paragraph was added. It begins "Let there be no hope for informers; and let all wickedness perish instantly." It asks God to cast down and humble "the dominion of arrogance," a phrase often applied to the oppressive Roman Empire. It concludes "Praised be Thou, O Lord, Who breakest the enemies and humblest the arrogant." Everyone present was expected to respond "Amen" at the end of this prayer. Since an informer would thus be joining in a curse upon himself, it was hoped that he would therefore stay away from the synagogue.

With slight variations in the text the paragraph remains part of the Orthodox prayer to this day; and The Eighteen Benedictions remains actually nineteen. With its plea for the destruction of wickedness it represents the only negative thought in the entire prayer. It was therefore given its place immediately preceding the petition for the reward of "the righteous, the pious, the true proselytes and all who faithfully trust in Thee."

The middle group of petitions is identical for all weekday morning, afternoon, and evening services except for minor additions on half-holidays and on fast days. On all Sabbaths and festivals, however, the thirteen petitions are replaced by a special prayer on the theme of the holiday observance. The Eighteen thus becomes a Prayer of Seven. Only on the New Year, when there are three festival benedictions, it is a Prayer of Nine.

The final three benedictions are again similar for all occasions. Traditionally, they are called benedictions of "Thanksgiving." Actually only the one next to the last, the eighteenth, entirely follows this theme: "We will give thanks unto Thee and declare Thy praise for our lives which are committed unto Thy hand, and for our souls which are in Thy charge, and for Thy miracles which are daily with us . . ." (*O-1*, p. 151).

The seventeenth is, in effect, a summary of the petitions for the acceptance of our prayers and for the re-establishment of God's service in Jerusalem. In Jewish tradition all important prayers end with a plea for peace. The final and nineteenth benediction is a prayer for peace. "Grant peace . . . to us and to all Israel, Thy people. Bless us . . . all of us together with the light of Thy countenance . . ." (*O-1*, p. 155).

At the end of The Eighteen it was customary in early days for the devout to add a prayer of their own. A number of these private prayers have been recorded in the Talmud. Some of them have been added, in the Prayerbook, as a silent meditation: "O my God! guard my tongue from evil and my lips from speaking guile; and to such as curse me let my soul be dumb . . ." (*O-1*, p. 157).

In the weekday morning service The Eighteen Benedictions are followed by confessional and penitential prayers beseeching the "merciful and gracious God . . . to forgive our transgressions" (*O-1*, p. 178). This section, known as "Supplications" (*Tahanun*), is, in turn, followed, on Mondays, Thursdays, and fast days, by the reading of the Torah accompanied by the prayers which mark the opening of the Ark, the taking out and the returning of the sacred scroll. Three men are called to the reading desk in succession. Each of them recites the blessings for the reading of the Law and a brief section of the portion of the week is read.

The "Adoration" forms the concluding section of each service. It gives voice to the hope for the day

when the world will be perfected under the kingdom of the Almighty, . . . when all the inhabitants of the world . . . know that unto Thee every knee must bow, every tongue must swear allegiance. . . . For the kingdom is thine, and to all eternity Thou wilt reign in glory; as it is written in Thy *Torah,* the Lord shall reign for ever and ever *(O-1,* p. 211).

The opening passage of the prayer sets forth the special duty of the Jews, who have not been made "like other families of the earth," to "bend the knee and offer worship and thanks before the supreme King of Kings, the Holy One, blessed be He, Who stretched forth the heavens and laid the foundations of the earth . . ." *(O-1,* pp. 208-11). The prayer was written by Rav, a Babylonian teacher of the third century. Originally it contained a strong condemnation of idolatry based on verses from Isaiah (30:7 and 45:20). "They worship vain things and emptiness, and pray unto a god that cannot save." During the Middle Ages, in Prussia, as late as the eighteenth century, the prayer was misinterpreted as a slur on Christianity and suppressed by government decree.

The final prayer in every congregational service—weekday, Sabbath, or festival, Orthodox, Conservative, or Reform—is the Mourners' *Kaddish.* It is recited by those who have recently lost a loved one or who observe the anniversary of a death. Some mourners attend the service for the sole purpose of reciting it. In some congregations, the mourners stand before the Ark to recite this prayer. In others, mourners rise while the rest of the congregation remains seated. In others, including many American Reform synagogues, the entire congregation rises in sympathy with those who mourn. Yet this is not a prayer of mourning. It is a sanctification of God. It is written not in Hebrew but in the rich and resounding Aramaic of the seventh or eighth century when it took its final form.

> May His great name
> Be mighty and holy
> In the world

His will has made.
May His Kingdom
Come to be
In your life, your days,
And in the life
Of the whole House of Israel;
May this be with speed,
And in a near time.
Amen.   (*Translation by Eli Siegel*)

This is its theme: There is no emphasis on death or life after death. It is a song of God's greatness, of man's duty to praise Him, of man's hope for peace on earth. Bereavement and sorrow tempt man to withdraw from God and the world. The comfort of faith helps him to face God and the world. He may not be able to understand the reason for his bereavement nor its meaning in his own life. But he feels that God wills what is good. Even though—no, because I cannot fully comprehend His deeds, "May His great Name be blessed forever and to all eternity."

The worshiper asks not to be removed from the pains of earth to the peace of heaven, but

May He who makes peace
In His high places,
Make peace for us,
And for all Israel.
And say ye,
Amen.   (*Translation by Eli Siegel*)

A person who is familiar with the morning prayer needs little additional information to understand the afternoon and evening services. These, too, have the Eighteen Benedictions as their central prayer. The afternoon service lacks the Call to Worship and the "Hear O Israel." These prayers recur, however, in the evening service. The section arranged about them ends with the petition: "Cause us, O Lord our

God, to lie down in peace and raise us up, O our King unto life . . ." (*O-1*, p. 373).

HOW WE PRAY

We know that God does not need our prayers. Our words of praise add nothing to His greatness. Even our petitions need not be expressed in words; for "He knows our needs before we utter them" (*R-1*, p. 349). Still, prayer has always been most important to man. The manner in which prayers are recited, the language, garments, and objects used in connection with prayer have been among the distinctive qualities of man's religions.

Most Jewish prayers were written for the congregation rather than for the individual. Jews have always taken seriously Hillel's admonition, "Do not separate yourself from the congregation." A group of ten men (*minyan*) must be present for congregational prayer. Some prayers, notably the Sanctification of the Eighteen Benedictions and the Mourners' *Kaddish*, are to be recited only when there are ten men present. The synagogue is the preferred place for prayer. But ten men gathered anywhere are a congregation suitable for joint prayer. And, whenever necessary, a man may pray alone—in his home, in the field, in a foxhole under fire, in a moving train. He still prays in the plural, to "our God" for "our salvation." For the Prayerbook unites all Jews into one congregation.

Attitude is important in prayer. Jews have always been careful to worship fully and properly dressed and physically clean. In biblical times prayers were recited with hands raised, palms up, toward heaven. Worshipers would frequently kneel and prostrate themselves with their faces to the ground. In postbiblical worship kneeling has been restricted to four occasions during the year—one on the New Year and three on the Day of Atonement. In Jewish practice, respect

is expressed by rising rather than by kneeling. The leader of
the congregation in worship—cantor, rabbi, or layman—
stands throughout the service. In Orthodox practice worshipers rise for the Call to Worship, the entire Eighteen
Benedictions, the opening of the Ark, the *Kaddish*. In Reform they also rise for the *Sh'ma* but remain seated during
The Eighteen, except for the Sanctification. Orthodox Jews
always stand facing east, toward Jerusalem, and their synagogues invariably are oriented with the Ark against the
east wall. Men and women worship separate from one another, with women frequently seated in a balcony overlook-
ing the men's section.

Special garments also play an important part in traditional
Jewish worship. Orthodox Jews never worship with uncov-
ered head, and the most pious among them wear a hat or
skullcap not only during prayer but every hour of day and
night. During daily, Sabbath, and festival worship they wear
a prayer shawl (*tallith*) and throughout the day, a special
undergarment (*tallith katan*) which, like the prayer shawl,
has fringes on four corners. During weekday morning services, in addition, phylacteries (*t'filin*) are worn on the forehead and the left arm. Reform Judaism has discontinued the
use of the prayer shawl, the phylacteries, or the head covering, except for some congregations where the rabbi wears a
prayer shawl.

The language of prayer is important. The Prayerbook was
written in Hebrew with the exception of a few Aramaic
prayers, notably the *Kaddish*. In Orthodox and Conservative
synagogues most prayers still are recited in the original Hebrew. They are sung or chanted by a cantor, often with the
assistance of an a capella male choir. Some are chanted an-
tiphonally by cantor and congregation. Many are read si-
lently, worshipers quietly moving their lips while their
bodies sway rhythmically back and forth in complete con-
centration. The Reform synagogue retains only a few pray-

ers in Hebrew, particularly the Call to Worship, the *Sh'ma,* and parts of the Eighteen Benedictions. The rabbi leads the congregation in worship reading most prayers in English. The role of the cantor is reduced in importance and is frequently transferred to the baritone soloist in the choir. Organ accompaniment and background music is freely used. Responsive reading by rabbi and congregation has replaced the antiphonal chants, and silent prayer is reduced to a few paragraphs at the end of the Eighteen Benedictions. The use of English prayers, of mixed choir and organ introduced by the Reform movement is also increasing among Conservative congregations and even in some synagogues which still consider themselves as Orthodox.

Prayer is the authentic expression of Jewish philosophy. The words of Jewish worship are based on our religion's basic beliefs. These principles were arranged systematically, from time to time, by the philosophers of Judaism, notably in the Thirteen Articles of Faith of Maimonides (see pp. 6-7). The Prayerbook reflects these principles as they affect the lives of our people and as they shape their hopes, their aspirations, and their values. The Prayerbooks used by the various groups in American Jewry reveal the lasting faith of the People of the Book as well as the evolving patterns of a living religion.

PART III

JEWISH HOLIDAYS

"You shall rejoice in your feast . . ."
—Deuteronomy 16:14

EVERYBODY LOVES A HOLIDAY

EVERYBODY LOOKS FORWARD to a day of celebration. Men and women, young and old the world over look forward to each holiday with joy. They think about it cheerfully before it arrives. They prepare for it with a will. And they remember it with gladness after it has passed.

Yet it is hard to tell exactly what it is that makes a day a holiday.

On a day of celebration we do not go to school or to work, as the case may be. But that alone does not make it a holiday. On a holiday we can sleep later or in some other way break the daily routine. We may go to bed later the night before, or rise unusually early for an outing. On most holidays we dress a little differently, a little better, a little more carefully, or a little less conventionally. We honor the day according to its spirit. But sleeping late or rising early, shining our shoes or dressing up in our finery does not make the holiday.

On holidays, as a rule, we eat better food, or special kinds of food. Eating well and eating certain kinds of food which we associate with certain celebrations help the holiday spirit, but they do not make it. The holiday is not in the eating.

On holidays we often visit relatives and friends or we go to theaters and concerts. We look forward to these visits or outings. They seem part of the holiday. They are part of it, but they are not *the* holiday. Also, on practically every kind of holiday (and particularly on religious holidays) we do certain things. We go through certain ceremonies or rituals which make the day solemn in its own way and different from all the other days. But these ceremonies and rituals alone, no matter how much they are part of the holiday, are still the outer garments, like wearing our best clothes and eating good food, to signify the holiday and to honor it. The real holiday, the spirit of the holiday is not in them.

Where, then, is one to find the spirit of the holiday without which the day would be only an ordinary day? Where does the spirit of the holiday reside?

Most holidays are the celebration of events so important that we want to remember them forever. The remembrance of a given event is the spirit of that holiday. A man who keeps a holiday without knowing the event which the festivity celebrates is like an uninvited guest at a wedding who knows neither the bride nor the groom. He cannot be truly festive. To enjoy a holiday fully one must know both the bride and the groom—one must know the event celebrated and why it is still of great importance to us who celebrate it. Only then can we enjoy the holiday as it should be enjoyed, fully.

And each holiday is different, for each holiday has its own character. And the better we understand the character of each holiday, the greater our enjoyment of that special day.

THREE KINDS OF HOLIDAYS

There are three kinds of holidays in our lives. First, there are *family holidays,* such as births and birthdays, engagements and weddings, confirmations and graduations, and various family anniversaries. All of these are personal and family affairs which we share in celebration with our kin or close friends. Family holidays are practically the same the world over.

Then there are the *secular holidays,* such as, in our country, Columbus Day, Armistice Day, Memorial Day, the Fourth of July, the birthdays of the great presidents who added a measure of freedom to the world.

But most important of all, and most significant to all people, are the *religious holidays*. These are observed in each nation by the followers of the various living religions, each observing the holidays of his religion.

Most of the religious holidays of the world are devoted to events in the lives of the founders of the different living religions. Christmas, for instance, celebrates the birth of Jesus of Nazareth, who became the founder of Christianity. There are similar holidays to celebrate the birth of Mohammed, the founder of Islam (Mohammedanism); the birth of Siddhartha Gautama, the founder of Buddhism; the birth of Mahavira, the founder of Jainism; and so on. Besides their birthdays, other important events in the lives of the founders of the various religions are solemnly celebrated.

The Jewish religious holidays differ from all the others: There are none which celebrate the birth of Abraham or Jacob or Moses. Nearly all Jewish religious holidays commemorate events of peace and freedom.

According to an old legend, all Jewish holidays are connected with the name of God. God, we are told, is known to Israel by Seventy Names, and each stands for a special attribute of the Creator, such as: His wisdom, His justice, His mercy, His loving-kindness, His love of peace, His love of freedom, and so on. And each of His Seventy Names is associated with a given holiday. Actually, if we include the weekly and monthly holidays, we celebrate more days than seventy each year, though the number varies a little, depending whether the celebrant belongs to the Orthodox, Conservative, or Reform branch of Judaism; for some holidays, as we shall see, are observed for a longer period by the Orthodox.

We Jews the world over have observed our holidays with great devotion for many centuries. Not all the holidays, of course, came into being at the same time. The Passover, commemorating the emancipation of the Jews from Egyptian slavery over three thousand years ago, is older by well over a thousand years than Hanukkah, which commemorates an event that occurred in 165 B.C.E. In the course of time the ceremonies and rituals of each holiday underwent great changes. And the changes were not the same in different parts of the world where Jews dwelt. The Jews in Israel today, for instance, celebrate many of the holidays quite differently from the Jews of the United States or of Eastern Europe. But however they may differ in ceremony and ritual, they are the same in spirit to all Jews.

And the religious holidays were and are a great unifying force that held and hold the scattered Children of Israel together and confirm their faith, expressed in the ecstatic: "Hear, O Israel, the Lord is our God, THE LORD IS ONE!"

THE SABBATH

Most holidays, throughout the world, come every year, usually on the same date or the same day of the week. They are called annual holidays. But the most important of all the Jewish holidays is welcomed *weekly*. This is the day of peace and rest, the Sabbath.

The Sabbath is not only the most frequent Jewish holiday, it is also considered the most sacred. The Sabbath alone, of all the holidays, is prescribed in the Ten Commandments:

Remember the Sabbath-day, to keep it holy. Six days shalt thou labor, and do all thy work, but the seventh day is the Sabbath of the Lord thy God. In it thou shalt not do any work—thou, nor thy son, nor thy daughter, nor thy man-servant, nor thy maid-servant, nor thy cattle, nor the stranger that is within thy gates. For in six days the Lord made heaven and earth, and all that is in them, and rested on the seventh day; wherefore the Lord blessed the Sabbath-day and hallowed it.

This, the Fourth Commandment, is the spirit of the Sabbath and is one of the great contributions made by Israel to mankind.

Before this Commandment was set down and observed, no nation on earth recognized a weekly day of rest. People worked day in, day out, all through the year excepting for annual and special holidays. The shepherd on the hill, the farmer in the valley, the weaver in the mill, the potter at the wheel, and the maidservant in the home worked without the break of a single day through all the long year.

Then the Jews, who had been slaves under the Pharaohs in Egypt, threw off their yoke of slavery. And Moses, their emancipator, commanded them to observe one day of rest each week. This Commandment was intended not only for the Jews who accepted the Law, but also included all the manservants and maidservants of other religions. It even included the work animals of the field. The Commandment of the Sabbath declared one day of rest in every seven for all who labored on earth.

How Old Is the Sabbath?

No one really knows when the Sabbath was first celebrated, but it is probably the oldest of all Jewish holidays. According to one legend, long before the world was created, God created the angels and the soul of Adam. And on the first Sabbath after their creation they assembled in the Seventh Heaven and sang: "It is the Sabbath unto the Lord! Let the glory of the Lord endure forever!" And according to another legend, there is an Angel of the Sabbath who sits upon a Throne of Glory, and on the Sabbath day myriads of angels dance before him and sing in praise of the day of peace and rest, which, they say, is a foretaste of the World to Come, when all the people of the earth will live in everlasting peace and every day will be the Sabbath.

In the days of the Kings, many centuries ago, the Sabbath was celebrated in Jerusalem with great ceremony and ritual.

And some of the earliest psalms were composed at that time and sung by the Temple choir on that day and in honor of that day, the Sabbath.

Not only is the Sabbath the only festival mentioned in the Ten Commandments, but it is also mentioned 106 times in the Bible—more frequently than any other holiday. And it is also honored in the Talmud, which is the Jewish encyclopedia of religious learning. In the Talmud there are two books devoted to the description of what may and what may not be done on the Sabbath. And in these two books a great number of stories are told to endear the Sabbath to those who keep it.

One story in the Talmud tells that when Moses went up to Mount Sinai, God said to him:

"I have a precious gift in My treasury, and I wish to present it to Israel."

"Is it the Ten Commandments?" asked Moses.

"I shall give them the Commandments too," said God. "But this is a different gift."

"Is it the Sacred Books of the Law?" asked Moses.

"I shall give them the Sacred Books of the Law also," said God. "But this is a different gift."

"Is it the Holy of Holies in the Temple of Jerusalem?" asked Moses.

"I shall give them the Holy of Holies in the Temple of Jerusalem," said God. "But this gift is even more precious."

"What can it be?" asked Moses.

"It is the Sabbath," said God.

Another story tells that on each Sabbath eve two angels accompany every Jew returning home from synagogue. One is a good angel, and the other is an evil one.

On entering the house and finding the Sabbath light burning, the table prepared for the Sabbath feast, the house bright and clean, and all the people in it cheerful and in a holiday spirit, the good angel calls out:

"May it be His will that it should be like this next Sabbath!"

And the wicked angel is compelled to whisper shame-facedly: "Amen!"

But if the house is in disorder and unprepared for the Sabbath, and the people are downhearted and quarrel among themselves, the wicked angel calls out gleefully:

"May it be His will that it should be like this next Sabbath!"

And the good angel is compelled to whisper sorrowfully: "Amen!"

There are many other legends about the Sabbath. According to one, so different is the Sabbath from the weekdays that with the appearance of the evening star on Friday (when the Sabbath day begins) the air becomes filled with a delicate fragrance no perfume can equal. But this fragrance is enjoyed only by those who observe the Sabbath and keep it holy.

This aroma even enters the food of the faithful and flavors it more deliciously than any known spice on earth.

The story is told of a Roman governor who once visited a great rabbi on the Sabbath day. After the governor had eaten the food offered him, he exclaimed:

"How good this food tastes!"

"It is the spice that gives the food its flavor," said the host.

"Then I must order a large quantity of this spice. What is its name?"

"It is named 'the Sabbath,' " the rabbi replied.

"I have never heard of a spice named the Sabbath," said the governor. "Where does it grow?"

"It is not an herb, and it does not grow," said the rabbi. "It is the day of rest, called the Sabbath."

"How is the Sabbath different from any other day?" the Roman governor mocked.

"How are you different from any other Roman?" asked the rabbi.

"The Emperor was pleased to honor me and he appointed me Governor."

"God was pleased with the seventh day of the week and He appointed it the Sabbath," the rabbi replied.

The Sabbath Is a Bride

The Sabbath begins with the Blessing of the Candles at home on Friday evening. At sundown, in the Orthodox Jewish home, or when the family gathers for the festive Sabbath eve meal, in the Reform Jewish family, the mother lights the Sabbath candles on the dining room table gleaming with its white cloth and best silver and china. She prays, "Praised be Thou, O Lord our God, Ruler of the World, Who has sanctified us by Thy laws and commanded us to kindle the Sabbath lights." There are at least two candles. Some antique Sabbath candelabra have room for three or five candles or oil lamps; some for seven—like the seven-branched *menorah* kindled in the days of Moses, in the Sanctuary of the Desert, and, in Solomon's time, at the Temple in Jerusalem. In some Orthodox homes two lights are kindled for the parents and one light for each of their children.

And the "Kindling of the Lights," according to one tradition, goes back to the time when God said to Moses:

Tell the Children of Israel that if they obey My command to light the Sabbath light, they will live to see Zion illuminated with a light ten thousand times greater than that of the sun. And though the light will be so great, it will not blind the eyes of man but enable him to see without difficulty all the way around the world. And all the nations of the earth will rejoice in that light.

After the blessing of the candles, the people go to the

synagogue, where the congregation welcomes the holy day by chanting: "Come, my friend, let us welcome the Bride Sabbath!"

And this is the reason why the Sabbath is called a "bride":

When God created the world, so runs an old legend, the Sabbath came before the Lord and said: "All things, O Lord, You created in pairs. But me, the Sabbath, You created single."

And God said: "Israel will welcome you as a bride each week. And each week you shall give Israel a foretaste of the peace and glory of the World to Come."

In the Fourth Commandment, God reminded the people of Israel that they are permanently betrothed to the Bride Sabbath.

After the synagogue services the people return to their homes to celebrate the first feast of the Sabbath. The evening meal begins with the Blessing over the Wine—symbol of God's manifold blessings beyond man's daily needs. The father recites the Sanctification of the Sabbath, the *Kiddush,* which commemorates the completion of Creation and the emancipation of the Jews from Egyptian bondage. He cuts a loaf of especially prepared white, twisted Sabbath bread, praising God "Who brings bread out of the earth."

The second meal of the Sabbath is eaten at noon, after the family's return from the Sabbath morning service at the synagogue. Orthodox tradition calls the Jew back to the house of worship for the afternoon service followed by study of the Bible or the Talmud. In accordance with an ancient custom the Hasidim, a pious sect of East European origin, prolong the joy of the Sabbath with yet another meal, called the Third Feast, eaten in the synagogue with special prayers and songs, just as the day ends and the new week is about to begin.

The importance of making each of the Sabbath meals into

a feast is stressed in the Talmud. And many stories are told
how the faithful, who make an effort to the very limit of
their means to prepare for the Sabbath, are rewarded.

In Orthodox Jewish homes the Sabbath is welcomed as a
bride; and the departure of the Sabbath is accompanied by
great ceremony. After darkness has fallen and the stars are
seen in the sky, the mother chants a welcome to the new week
and praises God for the dew of His heaven and the fat of His
earth, upon which we all depend.

The father, upon returning from the synagogue, gathers
his family around him for the *Havdalah,* the departure of the
Sabbath bride. A spice box is brought out, full of fragrant
spices. A glass is filled to the brim with wine. And a ceremonial candle of many wicks twisted together and used
especially for this occasion is lighted. Everyone is silent.
Everyone inhales the aroma of the spices. Everyone comes
near the candle. And all hold their fingers near the flame to
feel its warmth, to reflect its light, to throw great shadows
on the ceiling. The shadows, according to tradition, symbolize that the day is over.

Then the head of the family chants solemnly: "Praised be
Thou, O Lord our God, King of the Universe, Who made
a distinction between light and darkness, between the holy
and the profane, between the Sabbath and the days of the
week . . ." He dips the tip of the candle in the wine or pours
the wine on the wick over an ornate *Havdalah* dish held by
one of the children. The flame is extinguished. The Sabbath
is over.

And everybody feels a little sad at that moment, as one
feels when parting from a good friend after a joyful visit.

The Different Sabbaths

The Jews everywhere celebrate the Sabbath; and there
are differences in its celebration from country to country,
from region to region, sometimes from family to family.

Some religious groups observe the Day of Rest more strictly than others. To an Orthodox Jew the preparing of a meal, carrying as little as a coin or a handkerchief, driving a car, lighting a match, or even turning on an electric light—all are labor forbidden on the Sabbath. Reform Jews disregard these prohibitions and emphasize synagogue service and home ceremonial. Conservative Jews, likewise, have relaxed many of the traditional prohibitions.

There are special Sabbaths during the year that take on either a more festive or a more solemn nature.

There is the Sabbath of Repentance (*Shabbat Shuvah*) that comes between the New Year and the Day of Atonement and reflects the solemnity of these holy days. There is the Sabbath of Remembrance (*Shabbat Zahor*) recalling deliverance from persecution before the festival of *Purim;* and the Great Sabbath (*Shabbat Hagadol*) celebrating human freedom before Passover. There is the mournful Sabbath before the Ninth Day of Ab (*Shabbat Hazon*) which is dominated by the reading of Isaiah's vision of doom for a sinful people (Isaiah 1); and the Sabbath of Consolation (*Shabbat Nahmu*), just a week later, when worshipers hear the reassuring message, "Comfort ye, comfort ye my people . . . ," from the fortieth chapter of Isaiah.

(The Sabbath Service, see pp. 206-11.)

THE SABBATH IN SCRIPTURE

In the Story of Creation

Thus on the sixth day the heaven and the earth, and all their host, were completed. And on the seventh day God rested. And God blessed the seventh day and sanctified it, because on that day God rested from all His work. (Genesis 2:1-3)

In the Ten Commandments

Remember the Sabbath Day, to keep it holy. Six days shall you labor and do all your work; but the seventh day is a Sabbath to the Lord your God: on it you shall not do any work, you nor your son, nor your daughter, nor your manservant, nor your maidservant, nor your cattle, nor the stranger who is within your gates. For in six days the Lord made heaven and earth, the sea, and all that is in them, and on the seventh day He rested. Therefore the Lord blessed the Sabbath day and made it holy. (Exodus 20:8-11)

Other References

Exodus 16:22-30; 31:12-17; 35:2, 3. Leviticus 19:3, 30; 23:3; 24:5-9; 26:2. Numbers 15:32-36; 28:9, 10. Deuteronomy 5:12-15. II Kings 4:23; 11:5, 9; 16:18. Isaiah 1:13; 56:2, 4, 6; 58:13; 66:23. Jeremiah 17:21-27. Ezekiel 20:12-26; 22:8, 26; 24:23, 26, 28; 44:24; 45:17; 46:1-12. Hosea 2:13. Amos 8:5. Psalms 92:1. Lamentations 2:6. Nehemiah 9:14; 10:32, 34; 13:15-22. Chronicles 9:32; 23:31. II Chronicles 2:3; 8:13; 23:4, 8; 31:13; 36:1.

THE NEW MOON (*ROSH HODESH*)

The Jews instituted the weekly celebration of the Sabbath, and they also observed the monthly celebration of *Rosh Hodesh,* the beginning of the month.

From the earliest times we Jews have measured time by the lunar month, which is twenty-nine and a half days in duration. But aware that the sun year is three hundred and sixty-five days long, our ancestors added one lunar month to every second or third year to even up the record. They found that, by adding seven "leap-year" months to every cycle of nineteen years, they could accurately synchronize their lunar calendar with the solar year.

In earlier days the decision on whether a particular month was to have twenty-nine or thirty days depended entirely on observation of the moon. Whenever two reliable witnesses testified to having seen the first rays of the new moon, the constituted authority—the high priest or the Sanhedrin—

proclaimed the beginning of the new month and signaled it by the blowing of the ram's horn (*shofar*), in Jerusalem, by messengers and a telegraph system of semaphor and fire signals, to the provinces of Israel and to Babylonia.

The Palestinian patriarchs retained the right to announce the beginning of new months and to determine leap years until the fourth century, when they were forbidden by the Roman authorities to communicate with their fellow Jews throughout the empire. Therefore, in 359, Patriarch Hillel II published the rules for the calculation of the calendar in order that Jews in any part of the world would continue to observe their holidays on exactly the same dates, year by year. Ever since that time we Jews have reckoned time for our religious observances by Hillel's rules, and they have proven to be of amazing accuracy.

In Bible times the New Moon was celebrated by complete rest, special sacrifices, and festivities, much like the Sabbath. In postbiblical times, however, it came to be observed as a half-holiday distinguished mainly by special prayers in the synagogue, which are still recited in the Orthodox service of our day. Reform Jewish practice simply provides for the announcement of the beginning of a new month on the preceding Sabbath.

(For quotations from the Prayerbook turn to pp. 211-13.)

The Jewish Calendar

The days of the week, other than the Sabbath, have no names in Hebrew. They are simply known as "the first day," "the second day," and so on. Since there are no figures to represent numerals in Hebrew, the six days are represented by the first six letters in the Hebrew alphabet, used as numerals.

Strangely enough, every week in the year has a Hebrew name, derived from the first word in the weekly reading in the Five Books of Moses.

The Hebrew months are called: *Tishri* (September-October); *Heshvan* (October-November), *Kislev* (November-December), *Tebet* (December-January), *Sh'vat* (January-February), *Adar* (February-March), *V'adar* (the added month on leap year), *Nisan* (March-April), *Iyar* (April-May), *Sivan* (May-June), *Tammuz* (June-July), *Ab* (July-August), and *Elul* (August-September).

The Hebrew year is calculated from the biblical date of Creation, which is traditionally given as 3700 years B.C.E. According to this reckoning, September 26, 1957, will be the first day of the Jewish year 5718.

THE NEW MOON IN SCRIPTURE

On the day of your gladness also, and at your appointed feasts, and at the beginnings of your months, you shall blow the trumpets over your burnt offerings and over the sacrifices of your peace offerings; they shall serve you for remembrance before your God: I am the Lord your God. (Numbers 10:10)

Other References

Also Numbers 28:11-15. II Kings 4:23. Isaiah 1:13-14. Ezekiel 46:6-7. Amos 8:5. Psalms 81:4.

THE NEW YEAR (*ROSH HASHANA*)

All the people of the earth consider the beginning of each new year a holiday. But not all of them celebrate the New Year on the same day or even in the same season. There is no agreement when the year really begins. Some believe the year begins in the spring; and others claim that it starts with the end of summer. Up to the eighteenth century most Christians celebrated the New Year on the 25th of March, when winter was over and spring began. Many ancient nations considered the year ended when the summer was over and the harvest had been gathered. Their New Year came on the first day of autumn. The ancient Romans waited for the shortest day of the year, the winter solstice, and called that the New Year.

Though we Jews consider the month of Nisan, in the spring, as the first month, we celebrate the New Year, *Rosh Hashana,* on the first day of the seventh Jewish month, *Tishri,* which marks the beginning of autumn, following in the tradition of the ancient Egyptians, Persians, Phoenicians, and Greeks.

The New Year is also the beginning of a large group of holidays.

The first ten days of this holiday season are very solemn and are known as the Ten Days of Penitence. They are also referred to as the Days of Awe (*Yamim Nora'im*). Beginning with the New Year, they reach their climax, on the tenth day, with the Day of Atonement (*Yom Kippur*). So important are these two solemn festivals in the minds of most Jews that they are commonly called "the High Holidays."

Then follows the cycle of holidays that are gay. They begin with *Succot,* the Festival of Booths, and end with the happiest of all Jewish holidays, the Rejoicing of the Law, *Simhat Torah.*

The Book of Life

According to Jewish tradition, everything a person does is written down in the Book of Life. No deed, no word, no thought of good or evil goes unrecorded. And the record is kept by God in Heaven; or, according to one tradition, by Elijah the immortal Prophet, Keeper of the Records of the Deeds of Man.

On the New Year's Day the Book of Life is examined in Heaven. The good deeds and the bad deeds of the preceding year are weighed and judged. And finally the fate of each human being is decided upon and written down, "who shall live and who shall die; who shall attain the measure of man's days and who shall not attain it; who shall be at ease and who shall be afflicted; who shall be brought low and who shall be exalted."

This is why we Jews send *Rosh Hashana* greeting cards to each other, reading: "May you be inscribed for a good year!" (*"L'shanah tovah tikatevu."*)

Just as Christians everywhere wish each other a Merry Christmas and a Happy New Year whenever they meet during their holiday season, so Jews wish each other a Happy New Year during the *Rosh Hashana* season. Or they may express their good wish in the traditional Hebrew words, *"L'shanah tovah tikatevu."*

The Day of Judgment

There is, of course, a very good reason why the High Holidays are so solemn. And this is the reason: Although the fate of each person, for the coming year, is decided upon according to his deeds of the year before, the judgment in Heaven will be tempered with mercy for those who truly repent their bad deeds and evil ways, and who resolve to behave well toward all men in the future.

Jewish tradition has several names for the New Year's day. One of them is Day of Judgment (*Yom Hadin*); for men stand in judgment, on this day, not only before the Great Judge on High but each before his own conscience. Guided by the strict standards of justice in Jewish law, faithful Jews examine their past actions on this day. They search their hearts. They pray and they resolve to be good. They make New Year's resolutions.

The Day of the Trumpet Blast

Another name for the New Year's Day is the Day of the Trumpet Blast (*Yom T'ru'ah*). "On that day, the great trumpet shall be sounded . . ." The primitive sound of the ram's horn which is blown several times during the New Year's service reminds us again of the idea of judgment day. And it is indeed intended as an alarm, as a call to awaken man's conscience.

At the same time it is a call to the Judge on High, asking Him to forgive our sins for the sake of Abraham, who was willing to sacrifice his beloved son, Isaac, to prove his faith.

For in that dim, distant past God said to Abraham: "Because you have not withheld from me your son, even your only son, I will bless you and multiply your offspring like the stars of heaven and like the sand on the seashore."

According to the Midrash, Abraham then answered God: "In the days to come, should my offspring sin against You, remember this day. Remember that I was willing to sacrifice my son—and be merciful to them."

The ram's horn is blown on *Rosh Hashana* in remembrance of Abraham's and Isaac's readiness for sacrifice. We are reminded that sacrifice is necessary. God is asked, for Abraham's sake, to forgive our sins.

A Timeless Holiday

The story of Abraham and Isaac is important in the observance of the New Year's Day; but its remembrance is not the main feature of the holiday. As we shall see, almost every annual Jewish holiday is based on an occurrence in Jewish history: the Passover on the Exodus from Egypt; the Feast of Weeks on the Giving of the Ten Commandments; and so on. However, the two greatest festivals are independent of our people's history: the New Year's Day and the Day of Atonement are dedicated to the timeless problems of all men. They are devoted to every man's yearning for justice and for mercy.

On *Rosh Hashana* we worship God as the Holy King of all mankind Who is "exalted through justice and sanctified through righteousness." In one of the most solemn prayers of the day's long liturgy, we invoke God as "Our Father, Our King," acknowledging that we have sinned before Him, asking Him to erase the record of our guilt, to repeal the sentence that may be decreed against us, and to help us return to Him in perfect repentance. We beg Him to "inscribe us in the book of a happy life, of freedom and salvation, of forgiveness and reconcilation." We pray that "wickedness may vanish like smoke and the dominion of tyranny be removed." We give voice to the hope that "all Thy children unite in one fellowship to do Thy will with a perfect heart."

The major theme of New Year's Day is not, however, the fatalistic acceptance of God's decree. Just because God is just and merciful, He is always ready to wipe clean the slate of our guilt, provided we do our best to live by His laws. Even though our fate has been inscribed in the heavenly book, even though much of our lot is determined by the circumstances of our background and environment, "penitence, prayer and charity avert the severe decree."

Sweet as Honey, Clean as Water

Two picturesque ceremonials symbolize the Jew's hope for the New Year. When the *Kiddush,* the Sanctification of the festival, is recited in the family circle on the eve of *Rosh Hashana,* there is the usual cup of red wine as the symbol of God's bountiful blessings. The white Sabbath bread has been sweetened by the addition of a generous quantity of raisins; and the father gives to each member of the household a piece of apple dipped in honey with the prayerful wish: "May it be Thy will, O Lord our God, to renew for us a year full of goodness and sweetness."

Orthodox Jews observe the custom of going to a river or the seashore on *Rosh Hashana* afternoon. They cast breadcrumbs upon the water in order to symbolize that God will wash away the sins of all those who sincerely repent, just as the water washes away the small crumbs cast upon its waves.

Orthodox Jews observe the New Year for two days—even in Israel, where all other festivals are kept for one day only. And if the first day occurs on the Sabbath, this ceremony is postponed to the second day, just as the ram's horn is not blown on the Sabbath because it is considered work and for fear that it might accidentally break, and thus the Sabbath would be desecrated.

(For quotations from the Prayerbook, turn to pp. 213-15.)

THE NEW YEAR IN SCRIPTURE

The first day of the seventh month shall be a solemn rest to you, a memorial proclaimed with the blowing of the trumpets. You shall do no work of any kind on that day, but you shall bring a burnt offering to the Lord. (Leviticus 23:23-25. Numbers 29:1-6)

DAYS OF PENITENCE

Prelude and Interlude

When we Jews speak of the Days of Awe, we usually are referring only to the period beginning with the New Year. Our tradition, however, provides for a period of suitable preparation for these, the most important days in the religious year. From the first day of the month preceding *Rosh Hashana,* the month of *Elul,* the ram's horn is blown during the daily morning service to remind the worshipers that the time for repentance is near. In some communities penitential prayers, known as *S'lihot,* are recited throughout this month. Most Orthodox synagogues, however, arrange for special services for the recitation of these prayers where people confess their sins and plead for mercy to "The Lord, the Lord God, the God of mercy and forgiveness, slow to anger, abounding in goodness and truth, who extends His mercy to thousands and forgives transgression, iniquity and sin." In most communities, these *S'lihot* services begin on the Sunday before the New Year's Day. They are held before dawn—often right after midnight, the same hour when, according to tradition, King David would arise from his bed, strike plaintive chords upon his harp, and chant his penitential Psalms.

Repentance Means Return

The daily recitation of prayers of repentance continues in Orthodox synagogues after the two-day observance of the New Year. For though each man's fate for the coming year has already been written down in the Book of Life, the Judgment is not yet final. A contrite heart and a true confession of sin during the days before *Yom Kippur* may bring about a revision of the judgment. "The gates of prayer are sometimes open and sometimes closed," it is written, "but the gates of repentance are ever open."

The Hebrew word for "repentance," *t'shuvah,* literally means "return." To sin means to wander away from God. To repent means to turn back to Him; and God's arms are always open to welcome His returning children.

That does not mean that a man can repent during the Ten Days of Repentance and then go on sinning again and doing whatever evil may enter his mind. For he who says in his heart: "I will sin and repent and sin again and then repent again," from him the power of repentance is taken away.

There are no banquets, no personal celebrations during the Ten Days of Repentance. People go about making peace with their enemies and asking forgiveness of those whom they have wronged. For God will forgive transgressions against our fellow man only after we have done everything humanly possible to right the wrong which we have done.

On the Sabbath that comes during the Ten Days, known as Sabbath of Repentance, the worshipers in the synagogue throw themselves upon the mercy of the Lord and implore

This Torah mantle of embroidered red velvet and flower-brocaded panels was made in Germany in 1710. The Torah mantle makes a rich and dignified covering for scrolls of Sacred Law in the Torah Ark. *(Photo by Frank J. Darmstaedter, courtesy of The Jewish Museum)*

The Yemenite *Hanukkah* menorah pictured above is a rare ninth-century specimen of the ceremonial oil lamps used in the Festival of Lights. *(Photo by Frank J. Darmstaedter, courtesy of The Jewish Museum.)* The menorah below, shaped like an oak tree with graceful silver leaves, was made in Poland in the middle of the eighteenth century. *(Courtesy of the Hebrew Union College Museum)*

This is a modern refinement of the traditional candelabra, recently designed by Israeli artist Ludwig Wolpert. *(Photo by Frank J. Darmstaedter, courtesy of The Jewish Museum)*

...ight is a silver menorah ...n seventeenth-century Ger-...y. *(Photo by Frank J. ...rmstaedter, courtesy of The ...ish Museum, Harry G. ...dman Collection)*

At left is the Cup of Elijah, probably made in Vienna during the eighteenth century. Inlaid in gold leaf between glass is a biblical scene of the prophet. *(Photo by Frank J. Darmstaedter, courtesy of The Jewish Museum)*

At right, made in Bamberg in the eighteenth century, is a combination *Kiddush* cup and *Havdalah* candle. *(Photo by Schalita Studio, courtesy of the Hebrew Union College Museum)*

This handsome silver work was made in Vienna in 1815. The *seder* plate is used for the three pieces of *matzah* and for the symbolic food. The dominant figure is Moses. *(Photo by John D. Schiff, courtesy of the Hebrew Union College Museum)*

Above, probably from late seventeenth-century Holland, is
an elaborately engraved pewter plate used in the Festival of
Esther. *(Photo by Frank J. Darmstaedter, courtesy of The
Jewish Museum.)* Below is an Esther scroll with dramatic,
illuminated illustrations of the heroes in the queen's story.
This imaginative work was written and adorned by a Polish
scribe in 1748. *(Courtesy of the Hebrew Union College Museum)*

This striking silver case comes from Galacia, *ca.* 1750-
1760. The delicately wrought cylinder tells the *Purim* story
as beautifully as the parchment scroll of Esther which it
holds. *(Photo by Frank J. Darmstaedter, courtesy of The
Jewish Museum)*

David Holleman captures in dramatic mosaic illustration the "Legend of the Fox and the Angel of Death" from Louis Ginzberg's *Legends of the Jews. (Photo by Frank J. Darmstaedter, courtesy of The Jewish Museum)*

Him to banish all wickedness from the earth, so that all men
may live in justice and peace.

An Unusual Ceremony

The final twenty-four hours before the Day of Atonement
are spent in preparation for this most solemn of all festivals.
On that day some strictly Orthodox Jews still carry out the
only ceremonial which still follows the pattern of animal
sacrifice abolished with the fall of the Jerusalem Temple,
nineteen centuries ago. Where the custom still persists, a
rooster is obtained for each male member of the family; and
a hen for each female member. Of course, ducks and drakes
or geese and ganders may also be used. And if the fowl is
pure white it is considered a good omen.

When the father has gathered his family about him, each
holding his or her proper fowl, he and all the members
of the family chant a penitential prayer. And they ask God
the Merciful, that if it has been written in the Book of Life
that they should die the following year, to accept the fowl
in their hands as a vicarious sacrifice, and let them live.

After all the prescribed prayers are read, the feathers of
the neck of each fowl are singed and the ritual is over. The
animal is then slaughtered and the meat given to the poor.
Conservative and Reform Jews do not observe this custom.
In fact, the only ceremonial observance in the Reform Synagogue between *Rosh Hashana* and *Yom Kippur* consists of
special prayers for the Sabbath of Repentance.

The day before *Yom Kippur* is spent by many Jews in visit-
ing friends, neighbors, and business acquaintances, stopping
only long enough to shake hands, to ask their forgiveness,
and to wish them all an easy fast on *Yom Kippur* and a good
judgment when their fate is sealed in heaven.

Those who follow this custom prepare a supply of honey
cake. And a slice of this cake is offered to everyone who

comes to the house on the day before *Yom Kippur,* for honey
is the symbol both of the Torah and of peace.

(For quotations from the Prayerbook, turn to pp. 215-16.)

X   THE DAY OF ATONEMENT (*YOM KIPPUR*)

There is a tradition that the fate of each man, woman, and
child for the following year is written down in the Book of
Life on *Rosh Hashana.*

That fate is sealed on the last of the Ten Days of Repentance: *Yom Kippur.*

Naturally there is no day in the year as holy and solemn
to the faithful as the Day of Atonement, which is called the
Sabbath of Sabbaths.

When friends meet on the eve of this day, they greet each
other solemnly and say: *"L'shanah tovah techatemu!"* ("May
your fate be sealed for a good year!") And they look at each
other, wondering what fate has in store for them—the fate
that will be sealed for them the next day.

Then the eve of the Day of Atonement arrives.

The people gather in the synagogues, and that evening
and the entire of the following day are spent in fasting and
prayer. Many reasons are given for fasting. Self-discipline is
one of them. A second reason is that on the Day of Atonement one should concentrate completely on matters of the
spirit and pay no heed to the needs of the body. Also, by going hungry of our own free will we should feel sympathy
for those who suffer from hunger and want.

A person entering an Orthodox synagogue on Atonement
Day is impressed immediately by the white garments worn
by the worshipers. They are linen shrouds prepared by pious
Jews at the time of their marriage and worn, every year, on
this most sacred day in order to symbolize that all men are
equal as they stand before their Creator, even as they are
equal in death.

Even in Conservative and Reform synagogues where this ←
custom is not followed, the Ark curtain is white, the pulpit
cover is white and so are the mantles of the Torah scrolls.
White is the color of innocence. And white is the color of
the Day of Atonement, when worshipers hear the promise:
"Though your sins be as scarlet they shall become white as
snow" (Isaiah 1:18).

A Prayer and a Melody

The Atonement Eve service opens with a prayer known
as *Kol Nidre*. This prayer asks for the release from certain
vows and promises during the past year and for the year to
come. The haunting melody composed for this particular
prayer became the musical theme for the Atonement service,
and so it came to be known throughout the world. The
prayer and the melody remained part of the service. In the
Reform synagogue the *Kol Nidre* melody is retained, but
the words have been changed.

Confession, Memory, and Hope

Several times during the services of the day, the members
of the congregation repeat the confession:

For the sin which we have committed before Thee under com-
pulsion or of our own free will, knowingly and deceitfully,
openly or secretly. . . . For the sin which we have committed before Thee in speech, by sinful meditation of the heart, by spurn-
ing parents and teachers, by wronging our neighbor. . . . For all
these, O God of forgiveness, forgive us, pardon us, grant us
atonement.

Each member of the congregation recites his confession
personally before God. He receives pardon directly from
God. Each member is a priest in his own right. No religious
functionary stands between him and God.

Still, the confession asks forgiveness for "us," not "me,"

for the congregation as a whole, even for mankind as a whole. Though each man must make his own peace with God, must become "at one" with the Lord on the Day of Atonement, no man can stand entirely by himself. He feels bound to the human race and prays that "all Thy children may unite in one fellowship to do Thy will with a perfect heart."

There also is a strong feeling of unity with the past on the Atonement Day. And one of the most stirring parts of the day's worship is the memorial service when we pray for the peace of our dear departed and vow to honor their memory by our own good deeds.

The closing service of the day is a final appeal for God's mercy as the shadows of evening fall, as the Book of Life is sealed and as the heavenly gates of prayer are closed. There is a feeling of serenity, a triumphant sense of certainty that God has heard the prayers of all sincere worshipers and that He has forgiven in accordance with His promise.

The ram's horn is blown in one long, steady note.

The Day of Atonement is over.

People hurry home to break the long fast. They again wish each other a Happy Year. At home the table is set with good food.

That same evening, after the fast has been broken, some pious Jews begin to build the *Succah* for the Festival of Booths.

(For quotations from the Prayerbook, pp. 216-18.)

THE ATONEMENT DAY IN SCRIPTURE

On the tenth day of this seventh month is the day of atonement; it shall be for you a time of holy convocation, and you shall afflict yourselves. (Leviticus 16:29-34; 23:27-32. Numbers 29:7-10. Isaiah 58:3-7)

THE FESTIVAL OF BOOTHS (*SUCCOT*)

When a religion is very old (and Judaism is a very old religion) each celebration in it accumulates many meanings. As the centuries go by, so many important events occur that there are not enough days in the year to celebrate each one separately. That is why certain holidays really celebrate several events which took place in different periods.

Such a holiday arrives five days after *Yom Kippur*, on the fifteenth day of *Tishri*. It is called Succot, the Festival of Booths. It is also called Tabernacles. It is known, too, as The Feast of Ingathering. And more recently it has acquired, in Israel, the added name of The Feast of the Halutzim.

In the Bible and in the Talmud this holiday is often called simply the Festival.

A Feast of Joy After Days of Awe

The Midrash has an answer for those who ask: Why so many holidays in one month? When God led the Children of Israel out of Egypt, the rabbis tell us, He promised them a holiday each month. The first month He gave them Passover; the second, the students' holiday of *Lag B'Omer;* the third, the Feast of Weeks commemorating the giving of the Law. But then the people sinned by worshiping the golden calf. God punished them by withholding their holidays—the fourth, the fifth, the sixth month. As the seventh month, the month of *Tishri,* rolled around, God, in his mercy, forgave and—to make up for the festivals they missed—gave the Israelites not one but three festivals, *Rosh Hashana, Yom Kippur,* and *Succot,* the last in itself being three festivals in one.

It appears quite normal that after the solemn and serious Days of Awe we should feel like celebrating a joyful holiday —especially since we have so much to be thankful for in the autumn season. In fact, the Bible three times bids us to re-

joice on the Feast of Booths while even on the Passover rejoicing is commanded but once. The Midrash explains that
at the time of Israel's liberation many Egyptians were killed
at the Red Sea, and one should not rejoice at the downfall
of one's enemies. But at the Time of Ingathering everyone
has reason to be happy and to give thanks to God for His
bounty.

How the Festival Began

"In the fifteenth day of the seventh month, when you have
gathered in the fruit of the land, you shall keep a feast unto
the Lord seven days." When the Israelites settled in Canaan
after their long wanderings through the desert, they appre-
ciated the rich harvest of the fertile land. With field and
vineyards far from their village homes they would build
temporary booths for the harvest season. The harvest completed, they decorated the booths with fruits and garlands
and remained in them for a week-long festival of thanksgiving.

These booths also served as a reminder of the time when
they had left Egypt and had camped in the desert in make-
shift tents and booths made of animal skins or palm leaves
or wild olive branches or anything else they could find. Forty
years of living under such conditions was something which
the people were not likely to forget. The Bible would not
let them forget. "You shall dwell in booths seven days . . .
that your generation may know that I made the Children of
Israel to dwell in booths when I brought them out of the
land of Egypt."

And so remembering the wandering through the desert
became combined with the celebration of the Ingathering
of the Crops—a holiday very similar to the American Thanksgiving; in fact a double thanksgiving, both for the blessings
of the fields and the trees and for God's miraculous protection through the ages.

Throughout the ages Jews built their booths at harvest time—in their courtyards in the cities of the Roman Empire, on top of roofs in the crowded medieval ghettos, in the spacious gardens of American homes, in the courts of our synagogues, and even again in the fields and vineyards of Israel. They eat their meals and give thanks to Him who creates food for all mankind. They are grateful for God's protection as they look up through the latticed roof of the booth at the roof of God's wide, open sky.

The Palm, the Myrtle, the Willow, and the Citron

The *succah* or booth is by no means the only symbol of thanksgiving. Each *Succot* morning, excepting the Sabbath, the devout come to their booth or to the synagogue for a special ceremony. In their right hand they lift up a palm frond bound with myrtle and willow branches (called a *lulav*), and close to it, in their left, they hold up a flawless citron (called *etrog*). After pronouncing the blessings, they wave the *lulav* up and down and to all the cardinal points, east, west, north, and south. This is done to symbolize that God is everywhere.

There are many explanations as to what the palm, myrtle, willow, and citron of this ceremony represent. Of course they do represent all types of trees for which we should be grateful—giant palm and lowly willow, flowering myrtle and fruit-bearing citrus.

One tradition compares the four plants to human virtues: the tall, straight palm to uprightness and honesty; the myrtle to simplicity; the willow to sympathy; and the bright, fragrant citron to pleasantness and friendliness.

Then there is the legendary claim that they represent the four most important parts of the human body: the citron is the heart; the palm is the spine; the myrtle is the eye; and the willow is the mouth. When these four kinds of plants are shaken after the blessing, it is to remind the eye to see no evil, the mouth to speak no evil, the heart to desire no evil, and the spine to shudder at the very thought of evil.

The New Succot

An entirely new meaning has been given to this holiday during the current century in Israel. It began to be celebrated in honor of the pioneers (called *halutzim*) who went to Palestine to build argricultural colonies (called *kibbutzim*), to reclaim arid land, to irrigate deserts, and to drain swamps. The lives of these *halutzim* have been as hard as the lives of the Jews who wandered in the desert, many centuries earlier. Their protection from a host of enemies, their survival in the face of untold obstacles, has been just as miraculous.

A Day Is Added

In Orthodox and Conservative synagogues the first two days of *Succot* are observed as full festivals with solemn services and abstention from work. Reform Jews in America and all Jews in Israel observe only the first day in this manner. The rest of the seven days are considered half-holidays. Work is permitted, but special prayers are added to the daily synagogue service including a procession in which the *lulav* is carried and in which prayers and psalms are recited thanking God for His help in ages past and asking for His guidance in days to come. On the seventh day, known as *Hashanah Rabbah*, further prayers are added and the procession circles the synagogue seven times.

An eighth day has been added to the Festival of Booths, known as the Feast of Conclusion or *Sh'mini Atzeret*. The Bible simply states: "For seven days is the feast of booths to the Lord. On the first day shall be a holy convocation, . . . on the eighth day you shall hold a holy convocation; it is a solemn assembly; you shall do no laborious work." In postbiblical tradition, it has become the day on which we pray for rain and on which we recite special memorial prayers for our beloved dead.

(For quotations from the Prayerbook, turn to pp. 218-20.)

THE FESTIVAL OF BOOTHS IN SCRIPTURE

Exodus 23:16; 34:22. Leviticus 23:39-43. Numbers 29:12-35. Deuteronomy 16:13-15; 31:10, 11. Zechariah 14:16-19. Esra 3:4. Nehemiah 8:13-18. II Chronicles 8:13.

THE REJOICING OF THE LAW (*SIMHAT TORAH*)

After *Sh'mini Atzeret,* another day was added to *Succot,* a ninth day, and this is generally celebrated as the gayest of all Jewish holidays except, perhaps, the Feast of Esther. This holiday is known as *Simhat Torah,* the Rejoicing of the Law. In Reform synagogues *Simhat Torah* is combined with *Sh'mini Atzeret.*

The Five Books of Moses are divided into fifty-four portions, and each Sabbath a portion is read in the synagogues. It takes a year to read it all.

On *Simhat Torah* the last chapter of the Five Books is read. And then the first chapter of Genesis is turned to, and the reading for the year is started all over again.

On the Sabbath and on all other holidays the Torah is taken from the Ark only during the daytime. In many synagogues—Orthodox, Conservative, and Reform—the colorful Torah ritual of *Simhat Torah* is carried out both during the morning service and on the eve of the festival, in order to give everybody a chance to participate. All the Torah scrolls are taken from the Ark and are carried through the synagogue in a procession, with joyful chanting. Children participate in the procession carrying flags which sometimes are topped by apples and lighted candles. Not only the men of the congregation are called to the Torah, as the final chapter of the scroll is read, but all the children are permitted to recite the blessing thanking God for His great gift of the Law.

In many communities the children are given candy, nuts, raisins, and fruit to symbolize the sweetness of the Torah. In congregations following the traditions of the Hasidim a festive table is set up in the synagogue. The congregation remains to eat there. And then the dances start in honor of the Torah. In some places these dances last all afternoon and late into the evening.

Simhat Torah is celebrated with great joy because we Jews regard the Torah as our most priceless possession and God's greatest gift. While it is a serious book and contains many strict laws, we realize that its observance is the greatest source of happiness and of freedom. In a way, this feast of Rejoicing of the Law fits into the *Succot* atmosphere of thanksgiving—thanksgiving for the harvest of the spirit which is reaped by those who study the Torah and live by it.

In Scripture

Since this festival is postbiblical in origin, there is no mention of it in the Scriptures.

(For quotations from the Prayerbook, turn to pp. 220-21.)

THE FESTIVAL OF LIGHTS (*HANUKKAH*)

The Celebration of a Miracle

The first *Hanukkah* took place over twenty-one hundred years ago in Jerusalem, and was a time of great rejoicing.

When we think of what happened to cause that rejoicing, the joy today is just as great. For men's hearts never cease to delight in the triumph of the just over the wicked. And the joy is even greater if the just are only a few and seemingly weak, and the wicked are brutally strong and many.

This is what happened:

There was a tyrant in those days, a Syrian king named
Antiochus. He hated Jews and vowed to wipe their Faith
from the face of the earth. "Abandon your God!" he commanded. "Abandon your Faith!" said he. "Give up your laws
and your stubborn opposition to slavery and your ideas of
mercy and justice! And turn into Greeks or perish!"

The tyrant Antiochus filled the Temple of Jerusalem with
Greek idols, and the streets of the city he filled with desola-
tion.

He ordered the Holy Books burned, and with them all
those who tried to save the Books. He forbade the Jews to
raise their children as Jews. And wherever the tyrant's exe-
cutioners found a circumcized child, they killed him.

At that time there lived in Modin a righteous man named
Mattathias and his five good sons, as mighty as great oaks.
And when the king's men came to Modin and demanded
that the people offer sacrifices on the altar of false gods, Mattathias warned them:

"Though all the nations that are under the king's dominion obey him, and fall away every one from the religion of
their fathers, yet will I and my sons and my brethren walk
in the covenant of our Fathers."

When the king's men tried to force the people to obey,
Mattathias slew the soldiers, and the men weak enough to
obey them. Then Mattathias called out: "Whoever loves the
Law and maintains God's covenant, follow me."

Mattathias, his sons, and a handful of followers fled to the
mountains, and from their hiding places they harried the
king's soldiers. For years they made the life of the tyrant
Antiochus bitter with vexation.

At the death of Mattathias, his son Judah took his father's
place as the leader of his people. His battlecry was the phrase
from the Book of Exodus: *Mi kamoha ba*-elim *YHWH*
("Who is like unto you, O Lord, among the gods"). The
first letters of this clarion call (M-K-B-Y) compose the

word "Maccabee," and Judah and all his followers became known as Maccabeans.

The king gathered a mighty host to destroy Judah. And when the great army came down and the followers of the Maccabee saw them, they asked their leader:

"How can we, who are so few, fight against a multitude so vast and well armed?"

Judah answered: "If victory resided only in the multitude of a host, then we would indeed be lost. But our enemies come to destroy us for the price of the loot they can get, whereas we fight for our God, and our strength comes from heaven!"

Judah attacked the men sent by Antiochus; he made them flee, and he pursued them, and he destroyed them. Again and again the king sent his men against Judah and his handful of men, and each time the soldiers returned in defeat.

After many victories Judah and his men made their way back to Jerusalem, determined to rededicate the Temple. They cleaned the halls and they scoured the altars. But when the time came to light the Temple lamps, they found there was only one small cruse of sanctified oil for the eternal light, on the altar, which could not possibly last more than a single day. And it would take at least a week to properly prepare the pure olive oil for the holy lamps. Still, they rekindled the light, with the oil from the single cruse, to dedicate the sanctuary again to the service of God.

The next day they found the wick still burning brightly. And so on the second, the third, the fourth days.

And the oil miraculously lasted through eight days.

Hanukkah is celebrated for eight days to commemorate the miracle that happened in that little pitcher of oil which Judah found when he cleansed the Temple and which lasted for eight days to light the Temple lamps. And every year, since that first celebration, men gather in their homes to light the *Hanukkah* lamp.

They praise the Lord for delivering the weak out of the hands of the strong, the few out of the hands of the many, and those who live by the Law out of the hands of the wicked.

And they think not only of the fate of Antiochus and his hosts. They also think of other tyrants on earth who oppress the weak, impose their will on others, and threaten with extinction those who oppose their commands.

Hanukkah is a very gay holiday, celebrated primarily in the home. Gifts are exchanged. Good food is eaten. And in some families the children are given small, square spinning tops which have on their sides the Hebrew letters N, G, H, S. These letters stand for the words: *Nes Gadol Hayah Sham* (A Great Miracle Happened There).

Some people say that the great miracle refers to the cruse of oil that lasted for eight days. Others say that an even greater miracle happened there. For a few men of faith and courage triumphed over a mighty host full of corruption and wickedness. A few men were ready to lay down their lives for their right to worship in the tradition of their fathers. And they established the idea of religious freedom for all time to come.

And some people say that the great miracle of *Hanukkah* has not yet ceased to be. And that we, too, whenever we find ourselves in darkness and in sorrow may spin the top and take courage in the lesson taught us by Mattathias and his sons.

In Scripture

This festival is not mentioned in the Canonical Bible, but the story of its origins is given in the Books of the Maccabees in the Apocrypha.

(For quotations from Prayerbook, turn to pp. 221-23.)

THE NEW YEAR OF THE TREES (*HAMISHAH ASAR BISH'VAT*)

We do not think of Jews as a farming people. That is because for nearly two thousand years they were dispersed
throughout the world and for so long and in so many places
they were not allowed to own land or engage in any agricul-
ture. But in ancient Palestine the Jews were an agricultural
people. And in that land they treasured the olive tree, the
grape vine, and the date palm. The Bible encouraged them
to plant "all manner of trees," and forbade the destruction
of trees of a conquered land.

Trees were their good friends.

And just as the Jews believed that on the first day of their
seventh month each human being was judged and his fate
for the coming year was inscribed in the Book of Life, so also
did they believe that trees were similarly judged on the New
Year of the Trees, which comes on the fifteenth day of the
Jewish month *Sh'vat*—which is the first day of spring in that
part of the world.

The New Year of the Trees has never become a full holiday. Men work on that day. Children go to school. In Jewish
schools the day is remembered by singing songs and eating
fruit grown in the Holy Land.

As might be expected, this semiholiday has been associated
with tree planting a long time. In ancient Palestine it
was customary to plant a tree when a child was born: usually
it was a cedar for a boy, and a cypress for a girl. As the children and the trees grew up, the children cared for their own
trees. And on the New Year of the Trees special care was
given these trees. And when the children grew up and were
married, branches from their own trees were cut for the wedding canopy.

Today Jewish children throughout the world are encouraged to plant their own trees and to buy tree certificates,

which provide funds for the planting of trees in the State of Israel.

There is no particular service in the synagogue to take note of this holiday except that penitential prayers are omitted; nor is there any ceremony or ritual in the home, other than the custom of eating certain fruits and donating money for tree planting in Israel. In a general way this semiholiday symbolizes the Jewish remembrance and love of the Land of Israel.

THE FEAST OF ESTHER (*PURIM*)

Several Jewish holidays are associated with the name of a famed and good woman.

As part of the *Hanukkah* story we remember Hannah and her seven sons who became martyrs of the Jewish cause, and, according to one tradition, the apocryphal Book of Judith is read, recalling Judith's heroism in the defense of the fortress Bethulia. On the Feast of Weeks the story of Ruth, the faithful Moabite woman, is read; and on Passover we remember the part played in the Exodus from Egypt by Moses' sister, Miriam.

And *Purim*, the gayest of all the Jewish holidays, is the feast which honors a woman named Esther.

On this holiday people gather in the synagogues to hear once again the story of the Jewish girl who lived so many centuries ago, and through strange circumstances was chosen queen by the Persian King Ahasuerus.

The story of what happened to Queen Esther and her Uncle Mordecai and a wicked governor named Haman, is told in all its absorbing details in the Book of Esther. It is full of many fabulous incidents, of festivities on an unheard-of scale; of boasting and carousing; of plots of murder; of villains discovered just in the nick of time; of the king's life saved by the very man whom he unwittingly condemned to death; of how a wicked plan was hatched to destroy an entire nation on a given day; and how, not one second too soon, the wicked plotters were exposed and punished for their wickedness and the virtuous rewarded for their goodness.

The heroine of this book is Queen Esther, who saves her people from destruction by the evil Haman, son of Hammedatha. She is credited also with convincing King Ahasuerus to bring about peace and friendship among all the one hundred and twenty-seven nations over which he ruled.

The Book of Esther is one of the best of all mystery and adventure stories. To the faithful it is, of course, much more than a good story, which they never tire of reading. It is a great lesson in courage and faith.

Ever since the story of Esther was recorded, each time a calamity befalls the Jews, they remember the fate of Haman and his henchmen and their faith in ultimate justice is strengthened.

Purim is another holiday that has become a many-holidays-in-one. And it celebrates the downfall of all wicked plotters, from Haman to Hitler, and from the earliest to the latest enemies of the Jewish people.

In the synagogues, where everyone is usually expected to be very solemn and quiet, the children are given wooden noise-makers on *Purim,* and each time the name of Haman and his family and his followers are mentioned, they are encouraged to make all the noise they wish.

Purim is the welcome occasion for masquerades and carnivals, for dancing and merrymaking. Countless plays have been written through the centuries to be performed by children or adults. They all take their theme from the Esther story; and they all poke fun at tyrants of any time and of any place.

Purim foods include special delicacies such as *Hamantashen,* three-cornered cookies filled with fruit jam or sweetened poppy seeds. The cookie is supposed to be a replica of Haman's hat, but we know that it got its shape from the three-cornered hat of the medieval policeman and soldier, those petty tyrants who lorded it over the defenseless Jews.

Purim, since Bible times, has been a time for giving presents to children and gifts to the poor.

(For quotations from the Prayerbook, turn to pp. 231-32.)

PURIM IN SCRIPTURE

The *Purim* service is based on the Book of Esther (also called the Scroll of Esther, or *Megillah*). The entire biblical book is read as part of both evening and morning services. A modern version of Esther will be found on pp. 223-31.

FESTIVAL OF FREEDOM (PASSOVER)

The Great Emancipation

Early in spring arrives the most celebrated of Jewish holidays, Passover, which is really a double holiday. First, as the name suggests, Passover literally means "pass over," and celebrates the Holiday of the First-born. For when the tenth plague was visited upon Egypt and the Angel of Death was sent to smite the first-born of the land, he was commanded to "pass over" the houses of the Hebrews so that the first-born among them would be spared.

According to the Bible, this is how it happened: Moses went down to Egypt and said to Pharaoh, "Free my people, the Hebrews, from slavery; and let them go to serve our Lord!" But Pharaoh would not free the Jews. And though Moses performed great wonders before the king to prove that God had sent him, Pharaoh would not believe Moses.

God ordered Moses to punish the land of Egypt with many plagues until the king relented. Moses turned the waters of the land into blood. All the fish died, and the people suffered. Then the land became covered with frogs, and when the frogs died, "the land stank." Next the whole of Egypt became covered with lice, which afflicted man and beast. Swarms of flies filled the fields and houses. The cattle were stricken with pestilence. And the people became covered with boils and blains.

Still Pharaoh would not let the Hebrews go.

One day Moses stretched out his hand toward heaven, and it began to thunder and to rain. The thunder turned into fire and the rain into hail. And the fire, mingled with hail, smote man and beast and the trees and the herbs of the field.

A plague of locusts followed and devoured whatever the hail had spared. The locusts swarmed over the land in clouds and covered the fields. They left the fields bare and grassless.

Each time Pharaoh would plead with Moses to lift the plague, promising to let his people go. And each time Moses removed the plague, Pharaoh's heart hardened and he refused to keep his word.

Then God decreed the tenth plague. At midnight of the fourteenth of the month of *Nisan,* all the first-born in Egypt were to die. But the Hebrews who lived among the Egyptians were to be given a sign to place upon their doors so that the Angel of Death would "pass over" their homes and spare their first-born.

When Pharaoh heard of the tenth plague that was to come upon the land, he said: "It is better that one in ten should die than to let the Hebrews have their way."

But on the fateful night, when Pharaoh's own son was among those smitten, the king called Moses and pleaded with him to gather all his people and leave Egypt without delay.

So eager were the Hebrews to be delivered of their bondage that when Moses told them the king would let them go, they started out without any preparation and without taking any provisions with them other than the unleavened bread in their homes.

That is how Passover, which began as the holiday when the first-born of the Hebrews in Egypt were spared from death, became also the holiday of emancipation. In remembrance of the haste with which the Hebrews left Egypt, all future generations were commanded to eat unleavened bread for seven days.

In the long and fateful history of the Jews, there is not another event considered so important as their emancipation from Egyptian slavery and their leaving Egypt early on the morning of the fourteenth day of *Nisan,* many, many centuries ago.

Each Passover eve it is the duty of every devout Jew to imagine himself a slave in Egypt, redeemed by Moses out of his slavery.

The Symbolic Passover Meal

On the first night of Passover, a ritual is followed, called the *seder.* This ritual is given in a book, called *The Passover Story (Haggadah shel Pesach),* which every member has before him at the festivity. It is a beautiful story, full of wonders. And every home where the *seder* is strictly observed becomes a stage on which is re-enacted a great and ancient drama in which every member of the family takes part.

Early in this pageant the youngest member of the family rises to ask: "How does this night differ from any other night?" And the oldest member replies solemnly: "We were slaves to Pharaoh in Egypt, and the Lord redeemed us with a mighty hand." Other questions are asked, and the answers are given. Stories are told. Songs are sung. Four goblets of wine are tasted. A great feast is eaten.

In effect, the entire *Seder* service is one great symbolic meal and each of the courses has a special meaning. Like all Sabbath and festival meals, it is opened with the *Kiddush,* the Sanctification of the holiday with blessings recited over the wine and bread, except that on this night the bread is unleavened. Then parsley is dipped in salt water and eaten. The green parsley represents the rebirth of plant life in the new spring, the liberation of nature from the shackles of winter; and the salt water traditionally represents the tears of the angels for the Egyptians who perished in the Red Sea.

The ceremonial foods include a roasted egg, which, in tradition, became associated with death and sadness. In the *Seder* service it bids us mourn for the Egyptians who died at the Red Sea and for the destruction of the ancient Temple in Jerusalem.

The lamb bone is a reminder of the paschal sacrifice. The bitter herbs—usually horse radish—symbolize the bitterness of slave labor. A brownish mixture of apples, nuts, and cinnamon—called *haroset*—represents the clay from which the Children of Israel were forced to make bricks in ancient Egypt.

The festive dinner is almost like an interruption of the symbolic meal with its recounting of the ancient story of liberation, with its enumeration of the ten plagues, with its psalms of thanksgiving, its prayers and songs of gratitude for the many times in history when God led the Jews out of bondage into freedom. In many homes this service of freedom is extended until the rise of dawn.

The Unseen Guest

On the *seder* table you will always find one cup of wine over and above the number of guests. Usually it is a beautiful silver goblet filled to the brim. Nobody touches it throughout the meal. But during the service the door is opened for the unseen guest to whom this goblet belongs. It is Elijah, the biblical prophet. According to ancient legend, Elijah never died. He went to heaven in a fiery chariot, and he returns to earth, an eternal wanderer, to be with his people, to alleviate their suffering, and to strengthen their hope. He will appear, in the end of days, as the harbinger of the Messiah. It is expected that he will bring his message of eternal liberty for all mankind on Passover, the festival of freedom. The open door invites the homeless and hungry into our homes. It bids the messenger of freedom enter our hearts.

Seven Days Without Leaven

The *seder* unites the family in the home as the most significant Passover observance. In many congregations community *seder* services are held in the synagogue for those who cannot have a home service. Synagogue services are also conducted on the eve and morning of the first and seventh day in Reform congregations, and of the first, second, seventh, and eighth day in Conservative and Orthodox congregations.

While Reform Jews usually observe the biblical injunction to eat unleavened bread, called *matzah,* and to abstain from leavened bread for the seven days of the festival, Jewish tradition as observed by Orthodox and most Conservative Jews has extended the festival to eight days and has prohibited the use of any food product which might have been exposed to leaven. Therefore, all foods to be used in traditional homes during the Passover week—dairy products, wine, candy, canned goods—are prepared with the most careful scrutiny. The home is cleaned from attic to cellar. Special sets of dishes, pots, and pans take the place of the year-round utensils in the kitchen. A symbolic search for leaven throughout the house, with a lighted candle and a feather duster, concludes the elaborate preparations on the morning of the day before Passover.

(For quotations from the Prayerbook, turn to pp. 232-33.)

PASSOVER IN SCRIPTURE

The Passover observance is based on the events described in the first fifteen pages of the Book of Exodus. The festival itself is established by the ordinances in Exodus, chapters 12 and 13. The many additional references to Passover or the Feast of Unleavened Bread include: Exodus 23:15; 34:25. Leviticus 23:5-14. Numbers 9:2-5, 14; 28:16-25; 33:3, 4. Deuteronomy 16:1-8. Joshua 5:10-11. II Kings 23:21-23. Ezekiel 45:21-25. Ezra 6:19-22. II Chronicles 8:13; 30:1-27; 35:1-19.

SCHOLARS' DAY (*LAG B'OMER*)

Scholars' Day is a semiholiday which, by custom, has many pleasant associations. *Lag B'Omer* literally means "thirty-three in measure." For when the Jews were an agricultural people, they celebrated the gathering of the very first sheaf of wheat by bringing this first *omer,* the first "measure" as offering of thanks, on the second day of the Passover. Beginning with this day they counted forty-nine days—seven full weeks—and on the fiftieth, observed the Feast of Weeks. Orthodox and Conservative Jews still recite a blessing every evening between the second day of Passover and the Feast of Weeks and formally count the number of days elapsed. *Lag B'Omer* signifies that the festival occurs on the thirty-third day in this seven-week cycle.

The Bible does not refer at all to this particular holiday. However, a number of later legends explain its significance as the one happy day during an unhappy—or "unlucky"—period of seven weeks. It is said that a terrible epidemic claimed the lives of many students of Rabbi Akiba. On *Lag B'Omer* the epidemic suddenly stopped and the lives of Rabbi Akiba and the rest of his disciples were spared.

Another legend links the observance to a contemporary of Rabbi Akiba and to the miraculous survival of Judaism at a time of terrible persecution. Nearly two thousand years ago, after the Romans had conquered Palestine, destroyed Jerusalem, and completely razed the Temple, they forbade the Hebrew scholars to teach the Jewish law. They established the death penalty for anyone who was found breaking this prohibition. Among the scholars who refused to obey this edict was Rabbi Simeon ben Yohai. With his son he hid in a cave in Galilee, and there they studied for thirteen years, surviving on wild fruit and spring water. Many pupils came to visit their hermit teacher. They dressed as hunters and carried bows and arrows to avert the suspicion of the Roman soldiers. And when they came to their teacher in the cave, they remained for a while to study with him. When Simeon ben Yohai died—and he died on *Lag B'Omer*—he asked his disciples not to mourn his death but to make the anniversary a day of rejoicing. In Meron, Israel, Jews still observe *Lag B'Omer* with a pilgrimage to the place pointed out as Rabbi Simeon's grave.

Lag B'Omer is principally a children's holiday. Hebrew school students are taken out on picnics and hikes. Often they dress up as hunters and carry with them bows and arrows, as did Simeon's disciples. Since this is a festival in honor of Simon ben Yohai and Rabbi Akiba, in a number of cities it is observed as Jewish Book Day—to honor the scholars.

An unusual number of weddings take place on *Lag B'Omer*. For Orthodox Jews and many Conservative Jews consider it improper to get married during the "unlucky" days of "counting the *omer*." *Lag B'Omer* is the first day after the beginning of Passover on which marriages may be celebrated.

THE PENTECOST (*SHAVUOT*)

Seven weeks after the Passover comes the holiday which celebrates the receiving of the Tablets of the Law, called *Shavuot*, the Feast of Weeks, or Pentecost.

The number seven has many special meanings for the Jewish people. According to legend, seven things were created two thousand years before the Creation of the world.*
There are seven heavens. There are seven categories of dwellers in Paradise. A good man is clothed in seven garments of glorious clouds before he enters the gates of heaven. Seven times each night the cock crows to call the sluggards to waken, and thus gives them seven warnings that he who loves sleep must learn to love poverty. Man's life is divided into seven stages: infancy, childhood, boyhood, young manhood, the prime of manhood, middle age, and old age. The seven branches of the candelabra represent the seven days of the week as well as the seven great planets of the universe known to the ancients. And there are many other beliefs about the number seven.

But more important than seven is seven-times-seven. For seven-times-seven days passed from the time God freed the Jews from their bondage in Egypt to the time he made them free men forever through the Ten Commandments.

The holiday of *Shavuot* really completes the celebration of Passover. On the Passover the Jews were freed from bondage; and on Pentecost the freed slaves were made into a great nation when Moses received the Tablets of the Law.

The Jews believe that the Ten Commandments they received at Mount Sinai are so remarkable that, were all the

---

* 1. *Wisdom,* as given in the Five Books of Moses; 2. *Paradise,* for the benefit of the righteous; 3. *Gehinnom,* for the punishment of the wicked; 4. *The Two Thrones of Glory,* one for Justice and the other for Mercy; 5. *The Sanctuary,* the space for the Holy of Holies in the Temple of Jerusalem; 6. *The Name of the Messiah;* and 7. *Repentance,* for the redemption of the human soul.

people of the earth to abide by them, the world would be devoid of evil and become full of goodness.

There would be no theft.

There would be no murder or wars.

There would be no adultery.

There would be no lies.

There would be no envy.

There would be no idolatry.

There would be no worship of Mammon or other false gods.

There would be no taking of the Name of God in vain.

There would be no slavery.

It would, indeed, be a very good world to live in.

Shavuot is a holiday of many names. It is known as the Feast of Weeks; and it is known as the Season of the Giving of the Torah. It is also known as the Pentecost, meaning, in Greek, the Fiftieth, because it occurs on the fiftieth day after the beginning of Passover.

After the Jews settled in Canaan and began to tend their fields and orchards, they brought to their Temple the first fruits of the land which ripened at this time of year, and they called *Shavuot* also the Holiday of the First Fruits. And since *Shavuot* was also the time when the wheat and the barley was ripe for harvesting, it became known, too, as the Grain Harvest Festival.

Because *Shavuot* became also the Grain Harvest Festival, the custom arose to read the biblical Book of Ruth on this holiday in addition to the reading of the Ten Commandments from the Book of Exodus. It is the story of a Moabite maiden who embraced Judaism. She worked as a gleaner in the grain fields of Bethlehem. God rewarded her for her faithfulness, and one of her descendants became the famed King David of Israel. The reading on the Festival of the Ten Commandments of the story of Ruth, the convert, emphasizes the message of the Commandments not only to the Jews but to the entire world.

For many centuries it was customary in some countries to take boys to school for their first lesson on *Shavuot,* and the Ten Commandments were read to the new students as their first lesson.

Today, in all Reform synagogues and in many Conservative and Orthodox congregations, the confirmation of boys and girls who have completed their religious school training takes place on *Shavuot.* A new generation reaffirms its allegiance to the covenant of Mount Sinai, the Torah.

In Israel of today *Shavuot* is a very gay holiday. It is celebrated mainly as *Hag Habikurim,* the Festival of First Fruits. The streets of the cities and towns are decorated with flowers and green boughs. Youths march in parades carrying banners and singing songs. And the people who watch them join in their singing. Then the people gather in the squares to dance their joyful dances. And everywhere they eat food made with honey and milk—the twin symbols of the Torah and of the Promised Land.

It is a good and happy holiday.

(For quotations from the Prayerbook, turn to pp. 233-34.)

THE PENTECOST IN SCRIPTURE

The Season of the Giving of the Law is described in Exodus, chapters 19 and 20. The Decalogue is repeated in Deuteronomy, chapter 5. Other references to the Pentecost, or the Feast of Weeks, in the Bible include: Exodus, 23:16; 34:26. Leviticus, 23:15-21. Numbers, 28:26-31. Deuteronomy, 16:9-12.

FASTS AND FEASTS

When one speaks of fasting as a Jewish religious observance, he immediately thinks of the Day of Atonement. On that solemn day Jews abstain from all food and drink for a full day, from evening till evening. Fasting on *Yom Kippur* is a means of self-discipline. It demonstrates sympathy with the poor and the hungry. Abstaining from physical food emphasizes the dedication of man's entire being to the spiritual task of the Day of Atonement.

Orthodox Judaism decrees abstention from food and drink for similar reasons on various other occasions. No food is ever to be eaten before the morning prayer. Some pious Jews fast until noon on certain Mondays and Thursdays. Some fast on the anniversary of the death of their parents. Some observe the day before the new moon as *Yom Kippur Katan* —a Little Day of Atonement—to do penance for errors committed during the previous month.

Abstention from food is also practiced on days of mourning which commemorate calamities of the past. These fasts also are, in a sense, expressions of penitence. For it is an ancient belief that misfortunes are the result of transgression.

Thus, the ninth day of the month of *Ab*, the fifth month (July or August), is observed as a fast from dawn to sunset by most Orthodox Jews. On that day, known as *Tisha B'ab*, the first Temple was destroyed by the Babylonians, in 586 B.C.E. and the second Temple by the Romans, in the year 70 C.E. Legend has it that on the ninth day of *Ab* Moses descended from Mount Sinai with the tablets of the Ten Commandments and—seeing the Israelites dancing around the golden calf—smashed the precious tablets.

Many other misfortunes also are said to have befallen the Jewish people on that day. Orthodox worshipers recite the morning prayers sitting on the floor of their synagogues. The ornamental curtain is removed from the Ark and, in addition to a special Torah portion (Deuteronomy 4:25-40), a selection from the Prophet Jeremiah (8:13 to 9:23) and the entire Book of Lamentations are read in a mournful chant.

Dirges written on the occasion of medieval massacres are added to the liturgy.

Three other fasts commemorate events linked with the destruction of Jerusalem: the tenth of *Tebet* (December or January)—the siege of Jerusalem; the seventeenth of *Tammuz* (June or July)—the breach of her walls; and the third of *Tishri* (immediately after the New Year)—the murder of Gedaliah, which marked the end of Jewish independence under the Babylonians.

Fasts precede two of the happiest holidays: the fast of Esther, on the day before *Purim,* reminds of the fast ordered by Queen Esther when she risked her life to save the Jewish people in Persia, and the fast of the First-born, on the day before Passover, is an expression of thanks for the survival of the Jewish first-born when the Egyptian children died in the tenth plague, before the Exodus.

"Mourning Turned Into Joy"

Jewish tradition has applied to the fasts of national mourning the prophesy of Jeremiah: "I will turn their mourning into joy . . . and give them gladness for sorrow" (Jeremiah 31:13). In the days of the Messiah, when all mankind will be blessed with freedom and peace, the days of fasting will become festivals of rejoicing.

Independence Day—A New Festival

The achievement of political independence for the State of Israel has given Jews a refuge from oppression, and a reason for rejoicing. The fifth of *Iyar* has been celebrated as a holiday by the people of Israel and by their friends throughout the world ever since that country's declaration of independence on that day—May 14, 1948.

PART IV

ALL IN A LIFETIME

*"We will rejoice in Thy commandments forever;
for they are our life and the length of our days."*
—Prayerbook

JUDAISM, more than any other living religion, permeates the conscience of its adherents morning, noon, and night. On waking and on going to bed, when sitting down to eat or to study, in all his daily transactions and in all his relations with his family, the Jew is constantly reminded of his duty to God; and his behavior is prescribed by a fairly fixed code and ritual. From the moment he opens his eyes in the morning to the moment he retires for the night, every act is sanctified by prayer. But one cannot be a good Jew in thought and word only; he must prove them in deed. And the good deeds are also clearly defined.

And all his thoughts and words and deeds are predicated on one basic principle, which might be summed up as a *reverence for life.* "A person who has saved a single life is as though he had created the entire world." This talmudic statement reflects the profound respect for life which has always characterized Jewish thought. Life is a gift of God. Life, therefore, is sacred. All Commandments, save that of respect for God Himself, must be broken in order to preserve life.

Jewish practice demonstrates this respect for life at every important moment of a person's existence. Jewish rituals punctuate man's progress from the cradle to the grave, and each in its own way is a ceremony of consecration dramatizing the dedication of man's life to Him Who is the Creator of all life.

CIRCUMCISION (*B'RITH MILAH*)

The greatest miracle in human experience is the birth
of a child. With all our knowledge we still cannot cease
to wonder at the mystery of a new life coming into being.
The ancients were deeply stirred by this miracle of birth.
They were happy and grateful for God's gift, especially when
the child was a boy. At the same time they were afraid that
God might take away what He had given, and that the baby
would die in infancy. Therefore, sacrifices were brought to
express thanks to God, to implore Him for the child's life.
Some primitive religions even demanded that all first-born
males should be sacrificed to their deities in order to assure
the life of the parents and of later offspring. Jews felt that
God wanted His children to live for Him and not to die for
Him. Therefore, they instituted, instead of the sacrifice, the
symbolic dedication of the child to God in the circumcision
ceremony.

Abraham's Covenant with God

Many peoples in the Near East have practiced circumcision. The Egyptians are known to have practiced this religious rite from earliest times, though the explanations how
it originated are highly conjectural. They probably had a
vague knowledge of the hygienic value of this simple operation. At the same time they ascribed to it religious value as
they did to everything concerned with life and death.

According to the Bible, God has made a covenant with
Abraham and his descendants: "He that is eight days old
among you shall be circumcised, every male throughout your
generations" (Genesis 17:12).

This practice has been adhered to zealously as an essential
rite of Judaism. It was considered so important that it was
proper to perform this operation even on the Sabbath or on
the Day of Atonement—if this happened to be the eighth day

from the child's birth. The circumcision was frequently performed in the synagogue, where a special chair of honor, known as "Elijah's seat," was set aside for the godfather, who would hold the baby.

During the days of the Maccabees, and ever after when tyrants sought to destroy the Jewish faith by prohibiting circumcision, Jews zealously risked their very lives for the right to continue the ritual, which represented the first covenant between Abraham and God.

However, it was noted that in some rare instances children died after this rite because of loss of blood. The talmudists, some two thousand years ago, observed that some women, who themselves are immune, transmit to their sons a rare affliction, which we now call hemophilia, which often causes death through bleeding of any wound. They therefore made a rule that where parents lost two sons due to loss of blood in circumcision, they were forbidden to observe this rite for any of their sons born thereafter.

A Religious Custom

Nowadays most boys born in American hospitals are circumcised by their physician as a purely hygienic measure. Jews continue the ancient custom as a religious rite. It is a symbolic way of thanking God for the miracle of life and of dedicating the child to a life in God's service. It is a reminder that man's body is not so different from that of the animals, but that man's mind and soul can consecrate the body to do God's work on earth.

In Orthodox practice the ceremony is always carried out by a *mohel*—a man both learned in Jewish tradition and especially trained for this operation. Reform Jews often have a physician perform the operation while the family's rabbi or even the father recites the prayers.

The father presents his son for circumcision and gives thanks to God "Who has commanded us to make our sons enter into the covenant of Abraham, our father." The family and friends join in the prayer that the covenant may be fulfilled "by devotion to God's Law, by a marriage worthy of His blessing, and by a life of good deeds."

In some European communities the swaddling cloth used during the circumcision is embroidered with his name and with a Bible verse. On the boy's first birthday it is customary to present it to the synagogue, where it will be used to wrap the Torah scroll.

The Crown of a Good Name

There is a saying in the Mishna that "the crown of a good name" excels all other crowns, including the crowns of learning, of priesthood and even of royalty. While the Mishna refers mainly to a man's reputation, it was believed that a person's name was very closely associated with his character. Among Jews who follow Central and East European tradition, sons and daughters are usually named after a deceased relative whose memory the parents wish to honor. Among Jews from Spain and Portugal a son is often named after his father. In either tradition, similar given names remain in a family for centuries.

Many American Jewish families give their sons and daughters biblical names in their Anglicized forms. Others prefer to call their children by other contemporary names regardless of their origin; but they frequently add in the record a Hebrew name, in order to carry on the family tradition.

A boy is given his name at the time of his circumcision. A girl is named during a synagogue service. In Orthodox tradition the father is called to the Torah on the Sabbath immediately following his daughter's birth and a prayer is recited asking God's blessing on the newborn child and His help for the mother's complete recovery. In Reform synagogues the naming service is often delayed until both parents can attend a Friday night or Sabbath morning service.

REDEMPTION OF THE FIRST-BORN (*PIDYON HABEN*)

Among many primitive people, as among Hebrews in primitive times, all the first-born, whether of man, beast, or fruit, belong to God. And in our Bible we find the commandment: "The Lord said to Moses, 'Consecrate to Me all the first-born; whatever is the first to open the womb among the people of Israel, both of man and of beast, is Mine' " (Exodus 13:1-2). So great was the reverence for the mystery of life among the early Hebrews, that they would not derive advantage of anything first-born. First-born domestic animals were brought to the Temple as sacrifices. The first sheaf of wheat cut in the field, the fruit of a tree bearing for the first season, all belonged to God's Temple. First-born sons often were dedicated to the service of God. This tradition is clearly reflected in the biblical stories of Samson and Samuel.

At a very early period, however, Jewish law singled out the priests and Levites to serve God "instead of all the first-born among the people of Israel." First-born sons in families were "redeemed" by payment of money to the priest.

This ancient custom continues among Orthodox and Conservative Jews. On the thirtieth day after the birth of a first-born boy, a descendant of the ancient priests, known as a *cohen,* is invited to the home. The father presents his son to the visitor, who then asks: "Would you rather give me your first-born son or redeem him for five *sela* in accordance with the Law?" The father replies: "I would rather redeem him." The *cohen* receives the equivalent of five *sela* in silver, usually five silver dollars. He blesses the child and the family celebrates the occasion with a festive meal.

If the infant's father or mother is descended from priests or Levites, there is no need for the redemption ceremony.

A CHILD'S EDUCATION

The education of youth has always been one of the basic precepts of Judaism. *"Thou shalt teach them diligently . . ."* Jews knew that their people and their faith would disappear from the face of the earth if they failed to teach its precepts to their children. "The world exists by the breath of school children," says the Talmud.

In the Midrash we read that before God would entrust the Ten Commandments to the Jewish people, He asked them for a bond to guarantee their future observance. The Israelites offered their wealth as a bond. God refused. They offered their ancestors, Abraham, Isaac, and Jacob as a pledge. God refused. Finally they offered their children as surety; and God gave them the Commandments.

When, in the second century c.e. the Romans prohibited the study of the Law under pain of death, some friends advised Rabbi Akiba, one of the compilers of the Mishna, to save his life by ceasing to teach his students. Akiba responded by telling the fable of the Fox and the Fish: "The fishermen with their boats and nets are trying to catch you," said the fox to the fish in the lake. "Come ashore where I can protect you." But the fish replied: "If we are in danger in the water which is our element, how much more would we be in danger on land which is not our element?" The study of the Law is the element in which the Jewish people can best continue to live.

That is why the education of a Jewish child begins as soon as his eyes can enjoy the sight of the Sabbath candles and of the *Hanukkah* lamp; as soon as his tongue can taste the various holiday delicacies; as soon as his ear can distinguish and his mouth repeat the words of a simple prayer.

The formal training of the young Jew usually starts at the same time as his public school education. This is by no means a modern innovation. Two thousand years ago there was in

Palestine a well-developed system of primary and secondary schools. From the age of six, children would learn to read the Bible. Writing also was taught in these schools. Regulations provided that teachers must be well trained, that classes should not be overcrowded, and that the classroom should be as pleasant a place as possible. When a six-year-old child started school, they would give him a piece of honey cake on which the Psalm verse had been inscribed: "The ordinances of the Lord are sweeter than honey" (Psalms 19:10, 11). This was the youngster's first lesson.

There are many types of Jewish schools in America. The largest number of pupils attend religious schools associated with synagogues, Reform, Conservative, and Orthodox. Many of these, particularly in Reform congregations, are called "Sunday schools," offering two hours of instruction on a week-end morning. Additional classes are frequently held on weekday afternoons after public school hours. Some schools hold classes only on afternoons, three to five times a week.

In many communities several synagogues cooperate in sponsoring these afternoon Hebrew schools, while in other cities they are under the aegis of a Bureau of Jewish Education which is independent of the congregations. A small but increasing number of pupils in large cities attend Jewish schools all day, where they are taught all subjects required by the local public school system as well as Hebrew, Jewish history, the Bible, Jewish ceremonies and rituals.

Reform congregations emphasize the teaching of Jewish history, ceremonies, holidays, the Bible, and Jewish ethics—with English as the language of instruction; and relatively little time is spent in teaching Hebrew as a language. Conservative synagogues place greater emphasis on the teaching of Hebrew. Orthodox schools further stress the teaching of the Talmud. Schools sponsored by certain Zionist organizations concentrate on the teaching of Hebrew as spoken and customs practiced in modern Israel. Yiddish schools—decreasing in number—instruct pupils in the Yiddish language and its literature and in folk customs in the tradition of East European Jewry.

Education—at Home and in the Camp

Jewish educators do not limit their efforts to the classroom. Most congregations and most major communities conduct forums and institutes for adult education. These adult classes endeavor, principally, to enable parents to make their homes the seat of enlightened religious life and the normal source of religious knowledge for their children.

National and local organizations of Orthodox, Conservative, and Reform Judaism also sponsor a number of camps where healthy vacation fun is combined with religious education. Boys and girls from grade school through college may spend anywhere from two days to an entire summer at such a camp. In the informal camp atmosphere and in leisurely association with their rabbis and teachers they absorb the teachings of their faith in a pattern of everyday living.

BAR MITZVAH

As a child matures to adulthood he assumes more and more responsibilities, and these responsibilities are recognized by law. In most states in America a citizen gains the right to vote at the age of twenty-one. Males are subject to military service from the age of eighteen. Many states permit him or her to drive a car from the age of sixteen.

Jewish religious tradition similarly takes cognizance of a person's ability to assume more responsibilities as he goes through adolescence. Mosaic law considers a person an adult from the age of twenty and holds him liable for military service and taxation. Other religious duties, however, were incumbent on a person from an earlier age on. While the

Bible does not list these duties, the Mishna indicates that
"At five years the age is reached for the study of the Scripture; at ten for the study of the *Mishna;* at thirteen for the
fulfilment of the commandments" (Pirke Abot 5:24).

Centuries ago, when the Talmud constituted Jewish civil
law, a boy's father was responsible for his son's education, up
to the age of thirteen. By that time it assumed that he had
mastered the basic knowledge of Jewish life as found in the
Bible and in the postbiblical laws. From his thirteenth birthday on, a young man might be relied on either to continue
his studies on his own—and it was not uncommon for him to
do so until he had reached his twentieth year—or to learn a
trade. When a boy, on the Sabbath following his thirteenth
birthday, was called to recite the blessings over the Torah,
the father added the benediction: "Blessed be He who has
freed me from the responsibility for this child." Since the
Middle Ages a boy reaching the age of thirteen was called a
Bar Mitzvah, a talmudic term which means literally "Son of
the Commandment," or one obliged to observe the laws of
the Jewish religion.

Even though parents in our times still retain their responsibility for their child's needs long after he has reached the
age of thirteen, the *Bar Mitzvah* ceremony has assumed
greater rather than lesser importance in American Jewish
life. Many Orthodox and Conservative synagogues concentrate on the Jewish education of boys during the years just
prior to the thirteenth birthday. A boy is trained carefully
for his participation in the Sabbath service. The entire family and friends from far and near attend the service. The
Torah is taken from the Ark and seven or more adults, including the father and the close male relatives of the *Bar
Mitzvah,* are called to recite the blessings. The boy is called
last. He ascends to the pulpit, wearing a new suit with a
gleaming new prayer shawl about his shoulders. He chants
his blessings, usually reads a brief passage from the Torah;

recites the *Haftarah*—the reading from the Prophets for that particular Sabbath—and delivers a talk on the duties of a young Jew. A particularly proficient student may read the entire weekly portion from the Torah scroll and chant a major part of the service. The rabbi blesses the boy and conveys the congregation's good wishes to the family.

In many Jewish homes the *Bar Mitzvah* celebration is a major social event. Refreshments are served to the entire congregation after the Sabbath service; and a wide circle of family and friends are invited to a reception or a dinner at the family home or in a public hall. It is customary for the guests to shower the boy with presents.

Inasmuch as women are never called to the Torah in the traditional synagogue, the *Bar Mitzvah* ceremony has always been for boys only. With the number of girls studying Hebrew increasing, many Conservative and some Reform congregations—notably those under the influence of the Reconstructionist Movement—permit girls to go through exactly the same ceremony as a boy. This is known as *Bat Mitzvah,* "Daughter of the Commandment."

CONFIRMATION

In Reform synagogues and in some Conservative and Orthodox congregations the ceremony of confirmation is performed for groups of boys and girls, usually at the age of fifteen or sixteen. It takes place on the Feast of Weeks, which commemorates the receiving of the Ten Commandments. The confirmation class participates in the service by giving a series of brief talks or by presenting a religious pageant. They reaffirm their faith in God and their devotion to His Commandments, just as their forefathers proclaimed at Mount Sinai: "All that the Lord has spoken we shall do and we shall obey."

While the *Bar Mitzvah* observance dates from the Middle

Ages, confirmation was introduced into Judaism by the Reform Movement in Germany early in the nineteenth century. Jews had observed a similar ceremony performed by their Protestant neighbors and felt that its adoption in Judaism would give girls a greater share in Jewish education and practice. Most American congregations have delayed confirmation to the age of fifteen or sixteen, or the end of the tenth grade of public school, in order that boys and girls might obtain a deeper understanding of Jewish precepts than is possible at the age of thirteen.

Even though Reform Judaism was attacked by defenders of tradition for introducing confirmation into the synagogue, many Conservative and even Orthodox congregations subsequently instituted the ceremony. On the other hand, some Reform temples which abolished *Bar Mitzvah* in favor of confirmation later reintroduced it as an additional ceremony.

MARRIAGE (*KIDDUSHIN*)

In Jewish tradition marriage has always been considered both a sacred contract and the natural state for adult men and women. From the moment of Creation, God determined that "it is not good that man should be alone," and that "a man shall leave his father and his mother and shall cling unto his wife and they shall be as one flesh" (Genesis 2:18, 24). Judaism encourages early marriage. The rabbi in the Mishna who spoke of the age of five as the beginning of a child's education and the age of thirteen as the time for religious responsibility said that "at eighteen years the age is reached for marriage; at twenty for seeking a livelihood." It was not uncommon, in talmudic times and in the Middle Ages, for parents—particularly the bride's parents—to support a couple while the groom completed his higher education.

The Talmud considers the man who has no wife as "not a whole man." Jews have always felt that marriages were "for the sake of heaven," and also that marriages were made in heaven. According to the Midrash, a Roman lady once asked Rabbi Akiba: "What has your God been doing since he completed the work of creation?" Akiba replied: "He's been arranging marriages."

Until the end of the eighteenth century, marriages were usually arranged by parents—often with the help of intermediaries and professional matchmakers. The Jewish community did everything possible to encourage marriage. Where parents were unable to give a daughter the dowry, which was considered indispensable, providing such a dowry was considered one of the prime functions of communal charity.

The Talmud devotes two entire tractates to the subject of marriage. The tractate on Sanctifications (*Kiddushin*) deals largely with the ritual aspects of the wedding and the moral, legal, and social aspects of married life. The tractate on Marriage Documents (*K'tubot*) concerns itself with the marriage contract, especially with the protection of women's rights.

One Wife or Many?

Jews, like most people of biblical times and many Eastern people today, practiced polygamy—they had many wives. In the Bible many instances of polygamy are recorded. King David had a number of wives; and his son King Solomon had a thousand wives and concubines, according to the Bible. Polygamy was not formally prohibited by Jewish law until 1000 C.E. And even then the prohibition did not affect the Jews who lived among Arab nations where polygamy continued to be practiced. In 1948 the Jews who migrated from Arab countries to the State of Israel, where polygamy is forbidden, created a problem for themselves and the government of Israel with their more-than-one wives.

But even in Bible times Judaism considered marriage to

one wife preferable to polygamy. In the Prophets, in the Book of Proverbs, and in postbiblical Jewish literature we find many praises of monogamy, and the counsel to the husband to love his wife more than himself. He is cautioned, "Be careful not to cause her to weep, for God counts her tears." And they conclude that "He who weds a good woman is as if he had fulfilled all the precepts of the Law." And the Talmud concluded: "A man's home is his wife."

Civil and Religious Marriage

Marriage, in the United States as in most Western countries, involves both civil and religious authorities. The civil authorities issue a marriage license and thus authorize the marriage. The civil authorities authorize various persons to officiate at weddings—including rabbis, priests, and ministers. The civil authorities record marriages. A rabbi will not officiate at a marriage unless a license has been secured under state law. However, he may have to refuse to officiate even if a license has been obtained, because he must also comply with Jewish tradition.

A rabbi will not perform a wedding service on a Sabbath or a holiday. Orthodox weddings also do not take place during the period between Passover and the Feast of Weeks (except on prescribed days); and during the three-week period between the seventeenth of *Tammuz* and the ninth of *Ab*.

A Jewish marriage ceremony cannot be held for close relatives whose union is prohibited by Jewish tradition even though state law may permit it, such as between an aunt and her nephew, in accordance with the prohibition of Leviticus 18:12, 13, and 20:19.

A Jewish marriage ceremony cannot be held for a couple of whom one is not of the Jewish faith. Since marriage is the consecration of a Jewish home, it does not apply to a house divided along religious lines. There is no difficulty, however, if the non-Jewish party accepts the Jewish faith and is properly accepted as a convert to Judaism prior to the marriage.

The Marriage Service

The traditional Jewish marriage service opens with the officiating rabbi or cantor greeting the bride and groom with: "Blessed be he that comes in the name of the Lord." He prays: "O God, supremely blessed, supreme in might and glory, guide and bless this groom and bride."

There are two goblets of wine. The rabbi recites a blessing over each of them as a symbol of sanctification, and both groom and bride drink from both goblets. The first cup and the first benediction are part of the ancient engagement ceremony. Up to the eleventh or twelfth century this ritual used to take place months before the wedding. Since then this ritual has been combined with the actual wedding rites.

The groom then places the wedding ring on the forefinger of the bride's right hand and says: "Be thou consecrated unto me with this ring according to the Law of Moses and Israel." Sometimes an ornate ceremonial ring is used; but usually a simple gold ring is used. Orthodox practice prohibits the use of jeweled bands.

The marriage contract (*K'tubah*) is then read in Aramaic. This document, once an important legal protection to the wife in the event of her becoming widowed or divorced, now is used mainly to emphasize the moral obligations of marriage. "Be thou my wife according to the Law of Moses and of Israel. I will work for thee; I will honor thee; I will support and maintain thee, even as it becomes Jewish husbands, who work for their wives, and honor, support, and maintain them in faithfulness."

Seven benedictions are recited. A glass is broken by the bridegroom. The reasons for this ancient folk custom have long been forgotten. At the sound of the shattered glass everyone greets the newlyweds with: *"Mazal tov!"* ("Good luck!"). The groom kisses the bride and the wedding feast begins.

All Orthodox weddings are performed under a wedding canopy, called a *huppah*. This is a square piece of fine cloth, often beautifully embroidered. It is supported by four staves which usually are held by friends of the family. The *huppah* symbolizes the wedding chamber or the home which the bride and groom are about to build. When a wedding is held out of doors—and this was the prevailing custom throughout the Middle Ages—the canopy also protects the wedding party from the elements. Among the Jews who came from Spain or Portugal, called Sephardim, it is also customary for the fathers of the groom and bride to spread a prayer shawl over the young couple as a symbol of God's protection.

In the Reform marriage ceremony the use of the canopy is optional. The reading of the marriage contract, the second cup of wine, and the breaking of the glass are usually omitted.

To Have and to Hold

Sociologists have marveled at the stability of Jewish family ties. Until well into the twentieth century, Jewish parents had an outstanding record for taking care of their children; and Jewish sons and daughters had an equally good record for protecting their parents during their old age. In spite of the weakening of family ties in modern times this record has remained excellent among religiously observant Jews.

Of special interest is the relatively low divorce rate among Jews, particularly since the Jewish religion has always permitted divorce under many circumstances. Among the many possible grounds for divorce there were adultery, incurable disease, cruelty, ten years of childless marriage. Divorce action was initiated by the husband. But the wife could, for good reason, have the court force the husband to grant a divorce. Jewish divorce laws also protected the wife's property rights and determined custody of the children.

Orthodox and Conservative rabbis still follow the ancient practice of issuing religious divorce decrees, but only after every attempt at reconciliation has failed and after a legal divorce has been granted by a secular court. The divorce takes place before a rabbinic court of three rabbis and in the presence of witnesses. A scribe acting as the agent of the husband carefully writes the bill of divorcement (the *Get*), declaring, "You have been my wife until now; but now be released, set free, and put away so that you may be your own mistress in the future and may marry any man." The witnesses sign the document. The husband hands it to the wife, who in turn hands it to the presiding rabbi. He tears it across so that it may never be used again and retains it with the records of the court. In the United States a civil divorce must be obtained before securing a rabbinical divorce.

While divorce was always permitted, emphasis was on marriage as a sacred institution. The Talmud says: "If a man divorces the wife of his youth, the altar of God sheds tears on his account."

In Sickness and in Health

"Heal us, O Lord, and we shall be healed; save us and we shall be saved. . . . for Thou art a merciful physician. Praised be Thou, O Lord, Who healest the sick of Thy people Israel." Jews have always believed that healing of illness comes from God. At the same time they considered sickness as one of the real problems of life which challenge the religious, moral, and mental resources of man. God is the healer; but He has shown man rules of cleanliness and of moderation that he may remain healthy. God is the healer; but the physician is His co-worker. Faith in God and ardent prayer to Him help restore man's health, but not to the exclusion of proper medication.

The Bible and the Talmud abound with health regulations, many of which were most enlightened for their time. Medicine has always been a favorite profession among Jews. Throughout the Middle Ages a hospital was frequently built next to the synagogue as part of the religious and social institutions of the Jewish community. It has always been a religious duty to visit the sick and to pray on their behalf. While private prayers for those who are ill may be recited at any time, public prayers are said in connection with the Torah reading on Sabbaths and holidays.

A Jewish folk belief with regard to illness is reflected in the changing of names. When a person is seriously ill—particularly a child—the members of his family not only pray for his recovery but change his name. Favorite new names given to boys an such occasions are *Hayim,* which means "Life," and *Alter,* which means "Old." *Haya* and *Alta* are their feminine equivalents. The name is intended to be an omen that its bearer may live to grow old. The change was also intended to confuse the Angel of Death, for it was believed that this unwelcome messenger would look for a person of a certain name and, unable to find such a person, would pass the house.

DEATH AND BURIAL CUSTOMS

"Praised Be the Righteous Judge"

Rabbi Meir, a great teacher in the second century c.e., had two sons, and both died suddenly while their father was at the academy. The mother placed them upon a bed and covered them with a sheet. When her husband returned home from the academy at the end of the day, she said to him: "My husband, the other day someone left in my charge a treasure, but now he has returned to claim it. Shall I return it or not?" The rabbi said to her in surprise, "Is there any question about returning to the owner whatever he left with you for safekeeping?" She took him by the hand and led him to the bed where the two boys lay dead, and she removed the sheet from them. When he began to weep, she said to him, "The Lord has given and the Lord has taken away; blessed be the name of the Lord!"

This story illustrates the Jewish attitude toward bereavements. Life is a precious thing, which men hold in trust from God. He can reclaim it at any time. It matters not whether man wishes or does not wish for death, whether he understands or does not understand its cause. The truly religious Jew must believe that all of life is from the Lord and belongs to Him. Whenever God decides to claim a life, young or old, man must abide by God's decision. "Praised be the Righteous Judge," is the traditional response to the news of the death of a beloved person. "The Lord has given, the Lord has taken away, praised be the name of the Lord," is one of the refrains in the burial service.

When a Jew feels death approaching, he confesses his sins before God and asks for forgiveness. He closes his prayer with the affirmation of faith: "Hear, O Israel, the Lord our God, the Lord is One." If he dies suddenly or during unconsciousness, someone else recites the final prayer for him.

In Orthodox practice the task of preparing the deceased for burial is performed—as it has been for centuries—by members of the *Hevra Kaddisha*, the "Sacred Society." These are volunteers who cannot expect repayment or even a word of gratitude from the recipient in this life. While Reform and Conservative religious practice simply warns against excess in pomp and floral display at funerals, Orthodox Judaism rules out all flowers and all decorations. The deceased is dressed in a white linen shroud, acquired by him during his lifetime and worn during synagogue services on the Day of Atonement. He rests in an unadorned wooden coffin, his head on a bag of earth which may have been brought from the Holy Land. A man's face is covered with his prayer shawl.

Members of the Sacred Society keep watch until the time of burial, reciting prayers and reading from the Book of Psalms. The family and friends gather at the synagogue, at a funeral chapel, or at the cemetery for the funeral service. "O Lord, what is man that Thou art mindful of him?" Prayers emphasize the insignificance of man's life and the greatness of God. They express the faith that His decisions are wise even if they are beyond our understanding. They express confidence that He will bring rest and peace to the immortal soul of the departed and comfort to those who are left behind. "The Lord is my Shepherd, I shall not want . . ." "Thou wilt not abandon my soul to the grave; neither wilt Thou suffer Thy beloved to see destruction. Thou wilt show me the path of life. In thy presence is fullness of joy, at Thy right hand bliss forevermore."

The funeral service usually contains a eulogy recalling the good deeds of the deceased and reminding the bereaved that the memories of all that was fine and noble in the life of their beloved remain with them to comfort them even as his immortal soul lives on in peace.

The mourners and their friends follow the coffin to the grave. The coffin is lowered and earth is heaped on top of it. "Dust thou art and unto dust shalt thou return . . ." At Orthodox funerals a cut is made into a garment of each of the immediate family, or into a black ribbon attached to the garment. This symbol of mourning is derived from the ancient oriental custom of mourners tearing their clothes. The service at the grave closes with the recitation of the *Kaddish,* a prayer which exalts the name of God and expresses complete faith in His goodness.

While Orthodox custom insists on ground burial because of the literal belief in the resurrection of the dead and the literal acceptance of the statement "unto dust shalt thou return," Conservative practice countenances mausoleum burial, and Reform raises no objection against either mausoleum burial or cremation.

The belief in life after death has its roots in remotest antiquity. Several books of the Bible presume the continued existence of the dead in some shadowy form in the netherworld. There also was a belief in the resurrection of the dead "in the end of time." These ideas were developed further in the Apocrypha and the Talmud. As the Jewish religion became more and more concerned with the individual's relationship to God, there arose a more definite affirmation of the immortality of the soul and of judgment before the righteous God, either immediately after death or, at the time of resurrection, with the coming of God's kingdom.

Maimonides' eleventh Article of Faith states that "the Creator, blessed be His Name, rewards those who keep His commandments and punishes those that transgress them." The twelfth expresses "perfect faith in the coming of the Messiah." The thirteenth asserts "that there will be a revival of the dead at the time when it shall please the Creator." This continues to be the basic teaching of Orthodox Judaism.

Liberal or Reform Judaism affirms the immortality of the soul, accepts the idea of Divine righteousness beyond human understanding, and upholds hope in a messianic time of universal brotherhood and peace. It does not, however, maintain the doctrine of resurrection or of the coming of a personal Messiah.

Mourning Customs

Upon their return from the cemetery, the immediate relatives—husband or wife of the deceased, parents, brothers, sisters, children—seat themselves on low stools and remove their shoes. Orthodox and Conservative Jews observe this ancient expression of grief for seven days after burial, except on the Sabbath and on holidays. Reform Judaism simply advises mourners to remain at home for several days. Friends and neighbors visit the mourning family. They express their sympathy. They bring food for the family. They gather every evening and morning during the week of mourning to recite the daily prayers and read appropriate passages from the Bible or talmudic literature. On entering and on leaving the house of mourners, the customary greetings are omitted.

On the Sabbath or on a holiday which occurs during the week of mourning, the family attends synagogue services and there recites the *Kaddish* as an expression of their firm faith in God's goodness. Members of the family, particularly sons of the deceased, continue to attend services regularly in order to recite the *Kaddish,* and a memorial candle is kept burning in the home. Reform Judaism recommends a one-year period of mourning. Orthodox and Conservative Judaism observe an eleven-month period, based on a folk belief that the souls of the dead pass through the fire of *Gehinnom* immediately after their release from the body, in order to do penance for their sins; and that the prayers of pious children shorten the term of punishment.

Memorial Service

On the first anniversary of the funeral a headstone or marker is usually unveiled on the grave. During the first Memorial Day (called *Yahrtzeit*) a memorial candle is burned in the home for twenty-four hours, and the mourner attends synagogue service where he recites the *Kaddish* and makes charitable contributions in memory of the deceased; for "Charity saves from death."

Thereafter the anniversary is observed every year in a similar manner, with memorial prayers and contributions to charity.

DIETARY LAWS

Judaism, like many other religions, includes laws governing the foods which its adherents may eat and foods which they may not eat. These dietary laws are an important aspect of traditional Judaism. The permitted foods are called *kosher* or *kasher*, which in Hebrew means "to be fit"; and the prohibited foods are called *t'refah*, originally meaning "torn by a wild beast" but applied to foods prohibited for many other reasons. Many of the ordinances were originally hygienic measures, based on sound medicial observation; others are probably a carryover of ancient taboos. Throughout Jewish history these dietary laws kept Jews from associating intimately with non-Jews.

The dietary laws are divided into seven categories:

1. *Insects and creeping things*: All creeping things and all insects are prohibited as food, except certain kinds of locusts and grasshoppers.
2. *Prohibited fowl*: All birds of prey are forbidden as food.
3. *Prohibited sea food*: Fish that have both fins *and* scales are permitted; but they are forbidden if they lack either. Also prohibited are all salt-water and fresh-water crustaceans, such as crabs, shrimp, lobster, crayfish, and so on.
4. *Prohibited animals*: These are listed in Leviticus, chapter 11 and Deuteronomy, chapter 14. The animals whose meat may be eaten must have cloven hoofs *and* chew their cud. Cloven hoofs alone, or cud-chewing alone, does not make an animal kosher. The pig, a cloven-hoofed but not a cud-chewing animal, is especially singled out as being among the unfit-to-eat.
5. *Prohibited portions*: Since biblical times, the Jewish religion has prohibited the partaking of blood as food. The meat of kosher animals must be drained of blood and afterward salted and soaked in water in a prescribed way to remove every vestige of blood. In addition, major portions of the hind quarters of all kosher animals are also prohibited.

6. *Prohibition of animals improperly slaughtered*: Kosher animals must be slaughtered in the proper ritual manner (called *sh'hitah*), a quick severing of the jugular vein. After an animal is properly slaughtered, it is subject to careful inspection for signs of infectious disease. If any sign is found that indicates the animal suffered from an infectious disease, its meat may not be eaten. Animals that die from natural causes may not be eaten. Nor may one eat the meat of any animal killed by a wild beast—as indicated by the word *t'refah*.

7. *Prohibited mixtures*: A number of laws strictly prohibit mixing meat with dairy products. These ordinances are based on the verse: "Thou shalt not seethe the kid in the milk of its mother" (Exodus, 23:19). Milk and meat—or milk products and meat products—may not be mixed or eaten at the same meal. They may not even be cooked in the same utensils or served in the same dishes. That is why Jewish homes observing the dietary laws are equipped with two complete and carefully separated sets of utensils and dishes: one for meat and meat products; one for dairy dishes. Fish are "neutral" and may be eaten with either meat or dairy products. Six hours must elapse from the time meat has been eaten to the time dairy products may be eaten; a lesser period is allowed from the time dairy products are eaten to the eating of meat.

And there are long and complex explanations for each and every dietary restriction.

Orthodox Judaism maintains that the dietary laws are as fully binding today as they were in the days of the Talmud. Conservative Judaism permits a few relaxations of the laws for people eating outside their own homes. Reform Judaism does not consider the laws as binding, though many Reform Jews voluntarily observe at least part of the dietary traditions.

PART V

RITUAL OBJECTS IN JUDAISM

"You shall bind them as a sign upon your hand and they shall be as frontlets between your eyes."
—Deuteronomy 6:8

PART V

RITUAL OBJECTS IN JUDAISM

ALL RELIGIONS, in fact all movements in human civilization whose practices involve ceremonials of any sort, make use of certain objects which in time gain a ritual significance of their own. The Jewish religion is no exception. Various ritual objects are used in the Jewish home and the synagogue. Some of them are as ancient as the Bible; others became religious symbols in postbiblical times. Some are used universally by all observant Jews; others only by certain groups. Some are linked with certain holiday observances. Others have timeless significance.

The most important Jewish ritual objects are here arranged alphabetically:

ARK *(Aron Hakodesh)*

> The Ark, standing at or recessed into the east wall of the synagogue, contains the Scrolls of the Law. It is usually covered by a heavily embroidered curtain *(parohet)* or an ornamental door. Both Ark and curtain are based on the description of the Sanctuary of the Desert. (Exodus 25:10-22)

CANDELABRA *(Menorah)*

> Several types of candelabra are used in the Jewish home and in the synagogues. Most ancient in tradition is the seven-branched candlestick *(menorah)* which stands on the pulpit of most synagogues. It is described accurately in the Bible. (Exodus 25:31-40; 37:17-24. Leviticus 24:4) It has been used as an ornamental symbol of Judaism. It is found on the Arch of Titus in Rome and on ancient coins.

> An eight-branched candelabrum is used in the celebration of the Feast of Lights (see pp. 92-95). It is sometimes constructed in the manner of the seven-branched *menorah* but

often is built as a row of eight lights. The ninth, used to kindle the others, is located out of line. An ornamental shield forms the background of the lamp. Colored candles which burn for approximately thirty minutes are used in these candelabra. Sometimes oil and wicks are used.

There is also a variety of lamps used to welcome the Sabbath in the home (see p. 70). Many families use a pair of brass or silver candlesticks, for at least two lights should grace the Sabbath table. There are also Sabbath candelabra holding three or four candles. The medieval Sabbath lamp, a star-shaped brass oil lamp with five or six wicks, suspended from the ceiling, still is treasured as an heirloom in many homes.

Special candles braided from many wax-covered wicks are used for the *Havdalah* ceremony on bidding farewell to the Sabbath. Silver holders are sometimes used for these candles.

Another type of light is used as a memorial lamp. Glass-enclosed memorial candles are manufactured to burn for twenty-four hours on the anniversary of a death (see p. 133). Sometimes small electric bulbs are used as memorial lights in the home or in connection with a memorial tablet in the synagogue.

CANOPY (*Huppah*)

Since early postbiblical times a cloth canopy supported by four staves has been used to symbolize the wedding chamber during a marriage ceremony. Since marriages were invariably solemnized out-of-doors, the *huppah* also afforded protection against bad weather. (See pp. 96, 127)

CUP

A ceremonial cup, usually of silver, is used in the ceremony of consecration for Sabbath and holidays (*Kiddush*), both in the synagogue and in the home, when a blessing is recited over a cup of wine. It is also used at the farewell of the Sabbath (*havdalah*) and at weddings. The cup may have the shape of either a stemmed goblet or of a small beaker. It frequently shows rich ornamentation. Many families own and use a similar silver cup as the Cup of Elijah for the "unseen guest" at the Passover *seder*. (See pp. 102-03)

ETROG

A citron is used together with the *lulav* as a symbol of thanksgiving on the Festival of Booths, in accordance with Leviticus 23:40.

ETERNAL LIGHT (*Ner Tamid*)

A light is kept burning in the synagogue at all times. This lamp is usually suspended above the Ark. It is sometimes fed by oil; but usually, in American synagogues, it is an electric light. Often it is ornately decorated. It serves as a visible symbol of the eternal presence of the invisible God. The practice is based on the ordinance that a flame should burn perpetually in the sanctuary. (Leviticus 6:6)

HEAD COVERING (*Yarmulka, Kippah*)

A skullcap or other distinctive head covering is worn by traditional Jews at the time of worship, by extremely Orthodox Jews at all times. East European Jews frequently wear a wide-brimmed black hat; while members of the Hasidic sect wear a fur-trimmed hat on festive occasions. While there is no commandment in the Bible which makes the covering of the head compulsory, it was a custom taken for granted by most Jews. When the Reform movement abolished the wearing of the hat as a regional custom of the Middle East, and as without biblical sanction, they were bitterly attacked by Orthodoxy.

HUPPAH. *See* CANOPY

KIDDUSH CUP. *See* CUP

LULAV

One of the symbols of the Festival of Booths is a palm branch, tied together with three myrtle twigs and two willow branches. Held together with the *etrog* during worship, they are waved up and down, east, west, north, and south to thank the Lord of the world for His manifold blessings. The custom is based on Leviticus 23:40.

MAGEN DAVID. *See* STAR OF DAVID

MEGILLAH. *See* SCROLL OF ESTHER

MENORAH. *See* CANDELABRA

MEZUZAH

The word *mezuzah* literally means "doorpost." It refers to a parchment scroll fastened to the doorpost of a house or a room as the identifying symbol of a Jewish home. Usually protected by an ornamental case of metal, wood or plastic, the scroll contains two quotations from *Deuteronomy*: The *Sh'ma* (Deuteronomy 6:4-9) proclaiming love of the One God, and Deuteronomy 11:13-21, which emphasizes the importance of the Commandments, and the blessings found in obeying them. The *mezuzah* is based on the ordinance in Deuteronomy 6:9 and 11:20: "You shall write them on the doorposts of your house and on your gates." In the twentieth century, and particularly since World War II, it has become customary to wear a *mezuzah* as a personal ornament or symbol of identification.

MIZRAH

The word *mizrah* means "east" and refers to a marker placed upon the east wall of that room in the house in which prayers usually are recited, as a reminder of the proper orientation toward Jerusalem. The *mizrah,* usually a framed painting or piece of embroidery or needlepoint, contains the word *mizrah* in Hebrew, sometimes surrounded by appropriate Bible verses, sometimes against the background of a reproduction of the Wailing Wall in Jerusalem.

NER TAMID. *See* ETERNAL LIGHT

PAROHET. *See* ARK

PASSOVER PLATE

A special ceremonial plate is used by the head of the household as he leads the family in the *seder* service on the Passover eve. The more elaborate of these are constructed with three tiers for the three pieces of unleavened bread. The upper tier, often of silver or pewter, provides for compartments or separate containers for the various symbolic dishes of the feast. (See pp. 101-03)

PHYLACTERIES (*T'filin*)

Phylacteries are worn by Orthodox Jews during the daily morning prayer, not, however, on Sabbaths, holidays, and fast days. They are two cube-shaped boxes attached respectively to the left biceps and the center of the forehead by means of leather straps. Each box contains four quotations from the Pentateuch: Deuteronomy 6:4-9, 11:13-21; Exodus 13:1-10 and 11-16. The first deals with the love of the One God; the second with observance of the Commandments and their reward; the third and fourth with the redemption from Egyptian slavery. The four passages are written on one parchment scroll in the phylacteries for the arm, and on four separate scrolls in those for the head—in accordance with the distribution of man's five senses. For the wearing of the phylacteries symbolizes the voluntary subjugation of man's senses to the will of God. The custom is based on the literal interpretation of Deuteronomy 6:8 and 11:19: "You shall bind them as a sign upon your hands and they shall be as frontlets between your eyes."

PRAYER SHAWL (*Tallith*)

The prayer shawl is a rectangular, sheetlike garment, made of wool or silk, with a black or blue stripe and ornamental embroidery along the side which forms a collar. Four long fringes, knotted in a prescribed pattern and attached, one to each of the corners, are an essential feature of the prayer shawl, in fulfillment of the ordinance in Numbers 15:38-40. The *tallith* is worn by Orthodox and Conservative Jews during worship, especially the morning service on Sabbath and weekday. Traditionally it is used to wrap around the entire body and even to cover the head in order to shut out all outside influences which might disturb one's devotion. Frequently, however, it is folded and worn as a shawl about the neck and shoulders.

Inasmuch as the commandment to wear fringes on the corners of the garment is not limited to the time of prayer, Orthodox Jews also wear a special undergarment consisting mainly of a square piece of cloth with fringes affixed to the four corners, and known as *tallith katan*.

RAM'S HORN (*Shofar*)

The ram's horn is mentioned frequently in the Bible as a musical instrument used for signaling purposes. It is blown during the New Year's Day service and at the end of the Atonement Day service. (See pp. 78-79 and 86)

SABBATH CANDLES. *See* CANDELABRA

SCROLL OF ESTHER (*Megillah*)

The Book of Esther is inscribed on a parchment scroll and read during services for the Feast of Lots (*Purim*). Frequently an ornamental case is provided for the scroll.

SCROLL OF THE LAW (*Sefer Torah*)

For ritual use in the service, the Five Books of Moses (Torah, Pentateuch) are inscribed on a parchment scroll, by means of a quill pen with nonmetallic ink. The scribe (*sofer*) follows a set of exacting rules dating from the fifth century in order to assure exact copying of every sentence, every word, every letter, every space. The scroll is fastened to two rollers poetically called "Tree of Life" (*Etz Hayim*). Each scroll is provided with a band to tie it together, a mantle, often richly ornamented, to cover it, and a pointer in the shape of a hand. Most congregations also provide their scrolls with additional ornaments such as silver breastplates and crowns.

SEDER PLATE. *See* PASSOVER PLATE

SHOFAR. *See* RAM'S HORN

STAR OF DAVID (*Magen David*)

The six-pointed star, or hexagram, is a frequent ornament in the synagogue construction and in art objects identified with Judaism. It is the central symbol on the flag of the State of Israel. The star in the shape of two interlaced equilateral triangles was used as an ornament in many ancient cultures. Even though it is found on a Hebrew seal dating from the seventh century B.C.E., it was not prevalent as a Jewish symbol until it became popular under the influence of the Cabbalah, in the sixteenth century. At that time the term *Magen David,* literally "Shield of David," was first applied to the symbol, the six points of the star indicating that God is everywhere.

TALLITH. *See* PRAYER SHAWL

T'FILIN. *See* PHYLACTERIES

TORAH. *See* SCROLL OF THE LAW

PART VI

PRECEPTS, PROVERBS, AND FOLK BELIEFS

"I give you good precepts; do not forsake my teaching."
—Proverbs 4:2

OUR JEWISH HERITAGE is to be found in our Bible and the great commentaries on the Bible; in our long and stubborn history; in our holidays, mostly dedicated to the celebration of freedom; in our liturgy, mostly dedicated to the glorification of justice; and in our ritual and tradition in the adjustment to daily living. All of these are interrelated and inseparable. But the heritage would be incomplete without the treasury of precepts, proverbs and folk beliefs that reflect so well how our people think and feel about life in a world full of strife and confusion.

Long before the Books of the Bible were gathered and the Talmud sifted and edited, the Jews had already accumulated a great treasury of knowledge which was transmitted orally generation after generation. This oral knowledge even then consisted of precepts of behavior—what to do and what not to do in many human situations; observations reduced to proverbs, as guideposts to human inclination and the pitfalls to be avoided; and beliefs, a great variety of folk beliefs, some uncanny in their insight and others woven out of sheer superstition. All these were preserved by various literary devices to make them comfortable in our memories and pleasurable in repetition, until they became characteristic of Jewish thought and, consequently, behavior.

Many of the early sayings were incorporated in our Bible. Precepts such as, "You shall not follow a multitude to do evil" (Exodus 23:2), and proverbs such as, "Water wears away the stones" (Job 15:6) abound in all the Books of the Bible and serve as mentors in our daily behavior. Then there is the

Book of Proverbs replete with good advice and profound observation. By far the most numerous are the sayings throughout the Talmud and the early commentaries, called Midrashim, where we find a profusion of precepts, proverbs, and folk beliefs for every conceivable occasion. To these were later added many sayings, generation after generation. But the talmudic and midrashic sayings, in particular, have become a treasured part of our heritage.

We are including here a sheaf of these heritage sayings, limited to fifty precepts, three hundred proverbs, topically arranged, and fifty folk beliefs. These, we hope, will suffice to indicate the basic characteristics of Jewish epigramatic literature.

(The source of each precept, proverb, and belief included will be found on pp. 174-80.)

PRECEPTS

1. Do not believe the unbelievable; do not try to obtain the unattainable; and do not regret the irrevocable.
2. In a place where there are no men, strive to be a man.
3. Promise little and do much; and receive every man cheerfully.
4. Be deliberate in judgment; gain many disciples; and build a fence around the Law.
5. Rejoice not when your enemy falls; and let not your heart be glad when he stumbles.
6. Judge not the contents by the flask; a new flask may be full of old wine; and an old flask may not contain even new wine.
7. If you have done your friend a little wrong, in your eyes let it be great; if you have done him much good, in your eyes let it be little; if he has done you a little good, in your eyes let it be great; if he has done you a great wrong, in your eyes let it be little.

8. Let your house be a meeting place for the wise.

9. Provide yourself with a teacher; acquire a companion; and judge every man by his merits.

10. Do not befriend the wicked; move away from a bad neighbor; and never lose faith in justice.

11. Do not separate yourself from the group; do not trust yourself to your dying day; and judge no man until you have put yourself in his place.

12. Do not speak in riddles.

13. Respect your friend's property as if it were your own.

14. Be swift to please your elders, affable to youth, and receive all men with joy.

15. Never seek honor at the expense of another; nor carry a grudge until sundown.

16. Proclaim your virtues in a whisper, and your faults in a loud voice.

17. Be a lover of work and a hater of lordship; and do not cater to the ruling powers.

18. Let the honor of your friend be as dear to you as your own, and do not allow yourself to be easily moved by anger.

19. Do nothing which appears wicked in your own eyes.

20. Pray for the welfare of the government, for without it men would destroy each other.

21. Be suspicious of every government in power; for they who rule draw no man near except when it is to their advantage.

22. Make not the Law a crown with which to glorify yourself; nor a spade with which to dig.

23. For each good deed you gain for yourself one defender; for each evil deed you gain for yourself one prosecutor.

24. Do not try to appease your friend in the hour of his anger; to comfort him in the hour when his dead lie before him; to question him in the hour when he makes his vow; and to see him in the hour of his disgrace.

25. Be cautious in teaching, for to cause others to be wrong is worse than to be wrong oneself.

26. Deal tenderly with a sick or breeding beast.

27. Be deliberate in judgment.

28. Be searching in the examination of witnesses, and heedful lest your words lead them to falisfy.

29. Judge not alone, for none may judge alone save One.

30. Disqualify as either judge or witness: the dice player, the usurer, the flyer of doves (who wagers on the race), robbers, extortioners, and all suspected of dishonesty in connection with money.

31. Disqualify the witness who accepts payment to testify.

32. Do not condemn to death any man on the basis of a single witness.

33. It is the duty of both litigants to stand during the trial. If the judges wish to permit the two of them to be seated they may do so; but it is forbidden to permit only one to be seated, so that one stands and the other sits. Nor is it allowed for one to speak at length and the other to be told to be brief.

34. Rather be the cursed than the curser.

35. Do not hate anyone, for hatred leads to death.

36. Support the poor of the Gentiles with the poor of Israel, visit the sick of the Gentiles with the sick of Israel, and give honorable burial to the dead of the Gentiles as to the dead of Israel, because that is the way of peace.

37. Be strong as a leopard, light as an eagle, fleet as a hart, and strong as a lion, to do the will of God.

38. Perform charity in secret so as not to shame the recipient.

39. Forgive all insults.

40. Be soft as a reed, not hard like a cedar.

41. If you pray on behalf of another, while you yourself are in need of the same thing, your need will be answered.

42. When you pray, turn your eyes downward and your heart upward.

43. If you have it in your power to pray on behalf of your neighbor and fail to do so, you are a sinner.
44. If you direct your heart to God, your prayer will be heard.
45. Do not make a promise to a child which you know you cannot keep, for thereby you teach him falsehood.
46. Mislead no one deliberately, whether Jew or non-Jew, for injustice is forbidden against anyone, whether he belongs to our religion or to another.
47. Continue to hope, even within sight of the grave.
48. Avoid hatred, for he who hates a man is as if he hated God.
49. Be prudent in fear and remember that a soft answer turns away wrath and increases peace.
50. If you hear yourself abused and remain silent, you will be preserved from many abuses.

PROVERBS

Faith and Prayer

1. All men who do not worship idols are considered Jews.
2. One man is equal to the whole of Creation.
3. The gates of prayer are sometimes open and sometimes closed; but the gates of repentance are always open.
4. The good men of all races will inherit the World to Come.
5. Sin is a rebellion against God.
6. Before a man speaks, God knows his thoughts.
7. There is no sadness in the presence of God.
8. All is in the hands of Heaven, except the fear of Heaven.
9. He who attends a contest in which life is endangered scorns the Lord.
10. He who prays in a loud voice is of the prophets of falsehood.

11. Idolatory is synonymous with immorality.
12. Whoever repudiates idolatry is accounted a Jew.
13. Evil never comes from heaven.

Truth and Falsehood

14. Truth endures but falsehood does not endure.
15. Falsehood is common, truth is rare.
16. The path of truth leads to God.
17. God's seal is: Truth.
18. A liar should have a good memory.
19. The punishment of the liar is that he is not believed.
20. There are people who can lie even when they are silent.
21. The world is sustained by three things: truth, justice, and peace.

Justice and Peace

22. Upon what does the world rest? Upon a single pillar and its name is: Justice.
23. If you see a generation afflicted with many troubles, go and scrutinize the judges, for all the adversities which afflict the world are due to judges who abhor justice and pervert the law.
24. A judge should always imagine that a sword is pointed at his heart and hell (*Gehinnom*) yawns at his feet.
25. The sword came into the world because of delay and perversion of justice.
26. A judge may not accept a bribe of money; even a bribe of words is forbidden.
27. He who appoints an unfit judge is as though he had set up an idol.
28. No man shall die for the crime of another.
29. A judge is forbidden to listen to one party before the arrival of the other.
30. The law of the land is the law.

31. More important is a day of rain than the Resurrection of the Dead, since the Resurrection is for the righteous and not the wicked, whereas rain is for both the righteous and the wicked.

32. Whosoever takes a fee to adjudicate, his verdict is invalid.

33. Stealing from a Gentile is more serious than stealing from an Israelite, because it involves, in addition, profaning the name.

34. It is forbidden to take a bribe even to acquit the innocent or to condemn the guilty.

Wisdom and Folly

35. A wise man conceals his wisdom; a fool flaunts his folly.

36. Who is wise? He who learns from all men.
Who is strong? He who can control his desires.
Who is rich? He who is satisfied with his lot.
Who is worthy of honor? He who bestows honor.

37. Seven traits mark the wise and seven the foolish: The wise man does not speak before his superior in wisdom; he does not interrupt his friend's speech; he is not hasty in answer; he questions to the point and answers to the point; he speaks on first things first and on the last, last; regarding that which he does not understand he says, "I do not understand it"; and he always acknowledges the truth. The foolish have the opposite traits.

38. Better to share hell with the wise than paradise with a fool.

39. It is better to be the tail of a lion than the head of a fox.

40. Why are the fingers tapered like pegs? So that they can be inserted in the ears when one hears foolishness.

41. Even when folly succeeds it is still folly.

42. If one knot is unraveled, two knots are unraveled.

43. Silence is the fence of wisdom.

44. The wise say one word and mean two; hear one and understand two.

45. Silence is good for the wise; how much more so for the foolish.

46. He whose wisdom is greater than his deeds, what is he like? A tree whose branches are many and its roots few; for the wind comes and uproots it. But he whose deeds exceed his wisdom, what is he like? A tree whose branches are few and its roots many; so that even if all the winds blow upon it they do not move it from its place.

47. He whose good deeds are greater than his wisdom, his wisdom shall endure; he whose wisdom is greater than his good deeds, his wisdom shall not endure.

48. Men are more wont to be astonished at the sun's eclipse than at its unfailing rise.

49. Better a poor and wise child than an old and foolish king.

50. Neither the proud nor the angry have the power of prophecy.

51. If I am not for myself, who will be for me? And being for myself alone, what am I?

52. As you see a man, so he seems.

53. Not every man who succeeds in business is wise.

54. Silence heals all ailments.

55. New times, new men.

56. Even clever young people may grow up to be old fools.

57. The more you search, the more you marvel.

Virtue and Sin

58. Humility is the greatest of all virtues.

59. In a profusion of words there is room for transgression.

60. Happy is he who can ignore an insult; a hundred evils pass him by.

61. Who is mighty? He who turns an enemy into his friend.

62. Whoever runs after greatness, greatness flees from him; and whoever flees from greatness, greatness runs after him.

63. Whoever practices charity and justice is as though he filled the whole world with loving-kindness.

64. Even he who is maintained by charity must himself practice charity.

65. Charity is equal to all the Articles of Faith combined.

66. True charity is practiced in secret. The best type of charity is where the person who gives does not know who receives it; and the person who receives it does not know who gave it.

67. A name made great is a name destroyed.

68. If a man were to give his friend all the good gifts in the world but with a sullen face, it is ascribed to him as though he had given him nothing.

69. The door which does not open to charity will be opened to the physician.

70. The salt of money is in its diminution.

71. He who puts his neighbor to shame in public will have no share in the World to Come.

72. When the thief cannot steal he declares himself an honest man.

73. Envy, overindulgence, and hatred destroy a man.

74. Cleanliness leads to purity, purity to self-control, self-control to holiness, holiness to humility, humility to fear of sin, fear of sin to saintliness.

75. There is no suffering without iniquity.

76. Great is repentance, for it lengthens the years of a man's life.

77. He who says: "I will sin and repent and sin again and repent" will be denied the power of repentance.

78. If a man commits a transgression in secret, God proclaims it in public.

79. There is not a man upon earth so righteous that he has never sinned.

80. Everything is foreseen by God, yet freedom of choice is given to man.

81. The wicked are under the control of their heart; the righteous have the heart under their control.

82. Temptation leads a man astray in this world and testifies against him in the World to Come.

83. Temptation is at first like a spider's web, but in the end it is like cart ropes.

84. Temptation is at first like a passer-by, then like a lodger, and finally like the master of the house.

85. Temptation is at first sweet; in the end bitter.

86. The attribute of mercy exceeds that of justice by five-hundredfold.

87. Temptation is like a fly lodged between the two entrances of the heart.

88. Animals have no evil impulse because they have no moral sense.

89. Not the mouse is the thief, but the hole is the thief.

90. The associate of a thief is like a thief.

91. Slander slays three persons: the slanderer, the listener, and the slandered.

92. Whoever speaks slander is as though he denied God.

93. The evil impulse desires only what is forbidden.

94. All our deeds are recorded.

95. It is not in our power to explain either the prosperity of the wicked or the afflictions of the righteous.

96. From jesting to levity to lewdness.

97. One good deed leads to another; one evil deed to another.

98. He who commits an offense and repeats it, begins to believe that it is permitted.

99. A man is duty bound to pray for the bad, even as he prays for the good.

100. No person commits a sin unless there enters into him a spirit of madness.

101. A blessing is not experienced except in a thing over which the eye of a neighbor does not rule.

102. Generosity, humility, and kindness are the mark of a good man.

103. Had the Torah not been given to us for our guidance, we could have learned modesty from the cat, honesty from the ant, chastity from the dove, and good manners from the cock.

104. Envy, cupidity, and ambition lead a man to death.

105. Small transgressions lead to great offenses.

106. One self-reproach is better than many lashes.

107. Better one hour of good deeds in this world than the whole of life in the World to Come.

108. The place which the penitent occupy the righteous are unable to reach.

109. Not only he who sins with his body is called an adulterer; but he also who sins with his eye.

110. He who is not tempted and sins not is not virtuous; he who is tempted but sins not is virtuous.

111. Hatred is equal to the combined transgressions of idolatry, unchastity, and bloodshed.

112. To give oneself an air of superiority shortens a man's days.

113. Authority buries those who assume it.

114. He who gives vent to his wrath destroys his house.

115. The life of the irascible, the melancholy, or the overly compassionate is hardly worth living.

116. Do not become intoxicated and you will not sin.

117. Wine knows no secrets.

118. God hates the man who says "yes" with his mouth and "no" with his heart.

119. There are four kinds of tempers: he whom it is easy to provoke and easy to pacify, his loss disappears in his gain; he whom it is hard to provoke and hard to pacify, his gain disappears in his loss; he whom it is hard to provoke and easy to pacify is a saint; he whom it is easy to provoke and hard to pacify is a wicked man.

120. Whoever visits the sick takes away a sixtieth part of his illness.

121. Greater is he who follows the Commandments from love than he who follows them from fear.

122. There are four characters among men. He who says, "What is mine is mine and what is yours is yours," his is a neutral character; some say, "This is a character like that of Sodom." He who says, "What is mine is yours, and what is yours is mine," is a boor. He who says, "What is mine is yours and what is yours is yours," is a saint. He who says, "What is yours is mine and what is mine is mine," is a wicked man.

123. There are three crowns; the crown of wisdom, the crown of priesthood, and the crown of royalty. But the crown of a good name excels them all.

124. Every prophet prophesied only for the penitent.

125. More than the householder does for the beggar, the beggar does for the householder.

126. Charity saves from death.

127. A sacrifice atones only for one who sinned in error.

128. He who breaks a law to save a life is free of guilt.

Poverty and Riches

129. Poverty in a man's house is worse than fifty plagues.

130. Where there is no food, there is no study.

131. The world grows dark for the one who must depend upon the table of others.

132. A man takes greater delight in one measure of his own than in nine belonging to his neighbor.

133. Poverty causes transgression.

134. Grind with the teeth and it shows up in the heels.

135. A lion growls not in a den full of straw but in a den full of meat.

136. A rich man is he who derives pleasure from his wealth.

137. You can truly keep only what you have given away.

138. He who multiplies flesh, multiplies worms; he who multiplies property, multiplies anxiety; he who multiplies servants, multiplies lewdness; he who multiplies charity, multiplies peace.

139. Many are the friends at the palace gates; few at the gates of the debtor's prison.

Knowledge and Ignorance

140. The more knowledge the more life.

141. If you have acquired knowledge, what do you lack? If you lack knowledge, what have you acquired?

142. He who has knowledge will never lose his way.

143. The world rests on three things: the Law, service, and charity.

144. He who does not increase his knowledge decreases it.

145. Without knowledge there can be no understanding; without understanding there can be no knowledge.

146. To what is a scholar likened? A flask containing perfume. When it is opened the fragrance is diffused; when it is closed the fragrance is not diffused.

147. He who teaches the son of his neighbor is as though he had begotten him.

148. If one learns as a child, what is it like? Like writing with ink on clean paper. If one learns as an old man, what is it like? Like writing with ink on blotted paper.

149. Whoever learns the Scriptures and does not teach it, is like a myrtle in the desert.

150. The shy cannot learn; the irascible cannot teach.

151. An ignorant person cannot be pious.

152. An empty-headed man cannot be a sin-fearing man; nor can a shamefaced man learn; nor a passionate man teach; nor can one who devotes himself overmuch to business grow wise.

153. Not inquiry but action is the chief thing.

154. All theory and no practice leads to futility.

155. A man should not say, "I will study the Scriptures that people may call me learned; I will study Mishna that people may call me Rabbi; I will teach that I may be a Professor in the Academy."

156. Be considerate of the children of the poor, since wisdom issues from them.

157. A city in which there are no schoolchildren is doomed.

158. Where there is no knowledge, there are no manners; where there are no manners, there is no knowledge.

159. Study leads to practice.

160. The right thing can be said only at the right time, otherwise it is madness.

161. God weeps over three types of persons: over him who has the capacity to study but fails to do so; over him who has not the capacity for such study and yet engages upon it; and over him who rules the community with a high hand.

162. He who learns from the young, to what is he likened? To one who eats unripe grapes and drinks wine from the vat. And he who learns from the old, to what is he likened? To one who eats ripe grapes and drinks old wine.

163. A teacher should always be concise with his pupil, but never obscure.

164. The teacher should repeat the lesson until the pupil has learned it.

165. The maximum number of elementary pupils that should be placed under one teacher is twenty-five; if there are fifty, an additional teacher must be provided;

if there are forty, a senior student should be engaged to assist the master.

166. Why was the city of Bethar great? Because there were four hundred schools in the town of Bethar, in each of which were four hundred teachers, and each teacher had four hundred pupils.

167. There are four kinds of students: he who quickly understands and quickly forgets (his gain disappears in his loss); he who understands with difficulty and forgets with difficulty (his loss disappears in his gain); he who understands quickly and forgets with difficulty, he is a good student; he who understands with difficulty and forgets quickly, he is a poor student.

168. There are four types of students: the sponge, the funnel, the strainer, and the sieve: the sponge which soaks up everything; the funnel which takes in at one end and lets out at the other; the strainer which permits the wine to pass out and retain the lees; and the sieve which lets out the bran and keeps the fine flour.

Women

169. A woman of sixty, like a girl of six, runs to the sound of the timbrel.

170. A woman spins even while she talks.

171. Women are compassionate.

172. Women are light-minded.

173. Ten measures of speech descended to the world; women took nine and men one.

174. He who pays money to a woman, counting it from his hand into hers for the sake of gazing at her, even if he is as good as Moses, he will not escape punishment.

175. A man should walk behind a lion rather than behind a woman.

176. One cup of wine is good for a woman; two are degrading; three induce her to act like an immoral woman;

and four cause her to lose all self-respect and sense of shame.

177. A woman cannot act as a judge.
178. A good wife is half the income.
179. The things for which a woman longs are adornments.
180. It is not a woman's way to sit at home idle.
181. The goose bends its head while walking, but its eyes wander.
182. A woman has no heart for learning except in the use of the spindle.
183. He who multiplies gossip with women brings evil upon himself.
184. God endowed woman with more intelligence than man.

Marriage and Divorce

185. If your wife is short, bend down and whisper to her.
186. When a man's first wife dies it is as though the Temple had been destroyed in his lifetime.
187. Honor your wife and your life will be enriched.
188. Who loves his wife as himself, honors her more than himself.
189. A man's home is his wife.
190. Descend a step in choosing a wife.
191. Hesitate in selecting a wife.
192. One may sell a scroll of the Torah for the purpose of marriage.
193. Whoever marries a woman for her money will have disreputable children.
194. A tall man should not marry a tall woman lest their children be too tall; a short man should not marry a short woman lest their children be too small; a fair man should not marry a fair woman lest their children be excessively fair; a dark man should not marry a dark woman lest their children be excessively swarthy.

195. A man should sell all he possesses, if necessary, to marry the daughter of a learned man.

196. Everything goes wrong with those who are jealous.

197. Immorality in the house is like a worm on vegetables.

198. It is a religious duty to divorce a bad wife.

199. A man may not divorce his wife unless he has discovered her to be unfaithful.

200. A woman who has committed adultery must be divorced.

201. If a man vows he will not have intercourse with his wife, he is compelled to divorce her. A woman can also free herself from a distasteful marriage by vowing to withhold herself from her husband.

202. A man should spend less than his means on food and drink for himself, up to his means on his clothes, and above his means on honoring his wife and children.

Parents and Children

203. A parent should never make distinctions between his children.

204. It is forbidden to give a daughter in marriage while she is a minor.

205. A daughter is a vain treasure to her father. From anxiety about her he does not sleep at night during her early years lest she be seduced; in her adolescence lest she go astray; in her marriageable years lest she does not find a husband; when she is married, lest she be childless; and when she is old, lest she practice witchcraft.

206. One should honor his father in life and in death.

207. Happy is he whose children are sons and woe to him whose children are daughters.

208. A childless person is accounted as dead.

209. It is forbidden to have children in times of disaster.

210. A parent has no right to terrorize his children.

211. A parent should never threaten a child; punish him at once or say nothing.

212. If one refrains from punishing a child, he will end by becoming utterly depraved.

213. With children as with women: push them away with the left hand and draw them near with the right.

The Community

214. What is the responsibility of a man to his community? It may be likened to a company of men on board a ship. One of them takes a drill and begins to bore a hole under him. The other passengers say to him, "What are you doing?" He replies, "What has that to do with you? Am I not making the hole under my seat?" They retort: "But the water will enter and drown us all!"

215. A man must perform his duty to his fellow men exactly as to God.

216. Separate not yourself from the community.

217. Either companionship or death.

218. When the majority declare a thing permitted, it is permissible; when the majority declare against it, it is forbidden.

219. If you have entered a city conform to its laws.

220. A man should not depart from the established practice: when Moses ascended Mount Sinai he did not eat; and when the ministering angels visited Abraham they partook of food.

War and Peace

221. God created the world with peace.

222. The world is preserved by three things: the Law, justice, and peace.

223. Seven qualities avail before God: faith, righteousness,

justice, loving-kindness, mercy, truth, and peace—and peace outweighs them all.

224. Peace is equal in worth to all else in the world.

225. The mission of Israel is peace.

226. Be of the disciples of Aaron, loving peace and pursuing peace.

227. Thou shalt love thy neighbor as thyself.

228. Man was created a single individual to teach the lesson that whoever destroys one life, Scripture ascribes it to him as though he had destroyed the whole world; and whoever saves one life, Scripture ascribes it to him as though he had saved the whole world.

229. The soldiers fight and the kings are the heroes.

230. Even a bad peace is better than a good war.

231. When the ox is down, the butchers are many.

Work and the Worker

232. If need be, flay a carcass in the street and earn a living, and say not, "I am a great man and the work is below my dignity."

233. A man who has a trade is like a vineyard which is fenced in.

234. Seven years the famine lasted, but it came not to the artisan's door.

235. A man who does not teach his son a trade is as if he teaches him to become a thief.

236. Great is work, for it honors the workmen.

237. A man dies only through idleness.

238. Blessings only alight upon the work of a man's hands.

239. It is not your duty to complete the work; but neither are you free to desist from it.

240. According to the labor is the reward.

241. He who does not work shall not eat.

242. Idleness corrupts.

243. He who sleeps overmuch will be dressed in rags.

244. A man should not teach his son a trade which brings him into association with women.

245. He who defers paying the wages of a hired laborer transgresses five commandments of the Torah; Thou shalt not oppress thy neighbor; Neither shalt thou rob him; Thou shalt not oppress a hired servant that is poor and needy; The wages of a hired servant shall not abide with thee all night until the morning.

246. One should not expect faithfulness in slaves.

247. Usurers are comparable to shedders of blood.

248. A man should not eat his meal before giving food to his animals.

Health and Cleanliness

249. Sleep at dawn is like a steel edge to iron.

250. An imaginary illness is worse than a real disease.

251. A wise man does not reside in a city in which there is no physician.

252. A physician for nothing is worth nothing; and a physician who is far away is as much use as a blind eye.

253. One should wash face, hands, and feet every day out of respect for one's Maker.

254. It is forbidden to live in a city in which there is no bathhouse.

255. Bathing with hot water and not following it with cold water is like inserting iron into a furnace and not afterward plunging it into cold water.

256. Croup is like a thorn in a ball of wool which tears backward.

257. Three things do not enter the body, yet it derives benefit from them: washing, anointing, and exercise.

258. Physical cleanliness leads to spiritual purity.

259. Night was created for sleep.

260. Do not sit too much because it causes piles; do not stand too much because it is bad for the heart; do not

walk too much because it is bad for the eyes. Spend a third of the waking hours sitting, a third standing, and a third walking.

261. For good health: eat a third (of the capacity of the stomach), drink a third, and leave a third empty.

262. It is forbidden to sleep during the daytime more than the sleep of a horse.

263. Food induces sleep.

264. Three things weaken a man: fear, travel, and sin.

265. Better a drop of cold water (in the eyes) in the morning, and the washing of hands and feet in the evening, than all the eye salves in the world.

266. Bathe a baby in hot water and rub it with oil.

267. Rinse the cup before drinking and after drinking.

268. A person who despises the washing of hands before a meal is to be excommunicated.

269. Whoever eats bread without first washing his hands is as though he had sinned with a harlot.

270. He who prolongs his stay in the privy lengthens his days and years.

271. A wise man does not reside in a city in which there is no privy.

272. A sigh breaks half the body of a man.

273. A child should be taught to swim; it is a useful accomplishment and creates a liking for water.

274. Cleanliness is next to godliness.

Food and Medicine

275. Sixty runners ran but did not overtake the man who breakfasted.

276. If the patient says he wants something and the physician says he may not have it, the former is listened to. For what reason? The heart knoweth its own bitterness.

277. Where wine is lacking drugs are necessary.

278. To eat or drink standing shatters the body of a man.

279. While you are hungry eat; while you are thirsty drink.
280. Up to forty eating is beneficial; after forty drinking is beneficial.
281. Do not make a habit of taking medicine.
282. Wine enriches the blood.
283. One who is on a journey should not eat more than the amount customary in years of famine.
284. It is forbidden to cure oneself by means of Scriptural citations.
285. When wine enters, sense goes out.
286. The forbidden fruit which Adam ate was the vine, for there is nothing which brings so much lamentation upon man as wine.
287. Any food whose minimum standard is the size of an egg, the egg is superior to it as nourishment.
288. Dates give heat to the body, satisfy hunger, act as a laxative, and do not weaken the heart.
289. He who drinks water with his food will not suffer from indigestion.
290. Water is cheap and wine is dear; the world can exist without wine but not without water. Salt is cheap and pepper dear; the world can exist without pepper but not without salt.
291. He who wastes bread deserves to be poor.
292. Blessed be he who heals without fee.
293. Before a man has eaten he has two hearts; after he has eaten he has but one heart.

Death and the Life Hereafter

294. Would that life were like the shadow cast by a wall or a tree; but life is like the shadow of a bird in flight.
295. All brides are beautiful; all the dead are holy.
296. If the body is taken away, of what use is the head? If the house has fallen, woe to the windows!

297. This world is like a vestibule before the World to Come.

298. When a person is brought before the tribunal (after death) the first question put to him is: "Have you dealt honestly with every man?"

299. The fire of hell (*Gehinnom*) will never be extinguished.

300. The day is short, the work is great, the laborers are indolent, the reward is much, and the Master is urgent.

FOLK BELIEFS

1. If the first-born child is a daughter, it is a good omen for the males born subsequently.

2. A man only dreams the thoughts in his heart.

3. The eclipse of the sun is a bad omen for the whole world. If its face becomes the color of blood, it predicts war; if it becomes gray, it predicts famine.

4. Reading the inscriptions on tombstones causes loss of memory.

5. Ninety-nine die from the Evil Eye as against one from natural causes.

6. Longevity, offspring, and sustenance depend not upon merit but upon the planets.

7. The world is full of evil spirits.

8. Harmful spirits hide in wells, deserted fields, and in rains.

9. He who has an evil eye hastens after riches.

10. He who sneezes during prayer should regard it as a bad omen.

11. Change of name and change of place help to avert disaster.

12. A man should never open his mouth to Satan.

13. A horse may not go out on the Sabbath wearing a fox's tail or a scarlet band between the eyes.

14. The name of a person affects his career.

15. There is no reality in divination, but there is in signs.

16. If a verse comes to the lips when one wakes up it is to be regarded as a minor prophecy.

17. Even the curse of an ordinary person should not be treated lightly.

18. Five things cause the loss of memory: eating what has been nibbled at by a mouse or a cat; eating an animal's heart; eating too many olives; drinking water in which somebody has washed; and crossing one foot over the other while washing them.

19. Five things restore the memory: bread baked on coals; soft-boiled eggs without salt; frequent drinking of olive oil and spiced wine; and drinking the water left over from kneaded dough.

20. Honey and all sweet things are bad for a wound.

21. Radish is an elixir of life.

22. Five things are said of garlic: it satisfies, warms the body, makes the face glow, increases seminal fluid, and kills tape-worm. Some add that it fosters love and drives away enmity.

23. A hand which has not been washed on waking in the morning makes the eye blind, the ear deaf, and causes a polypus.

24. Who eats peeled garlic or peeled onion or shelled eggs or drinks diluted liquors, any of which has been exposed overnight, forfeits his life, and his blood is on his own head.

25. All raw vegetables make the complexion pale.

26. Horse-beans are bad for the teeth but good for the bowels.

27. Cabbage is good as nourishment and best as a remedy.

28. He who takes black cumin regularly will not suffer from pain of the heart.

29. He who eats small fish often will not suffer from indigestion.

30. To offset the harmful effects of lettuce, eat radishes; to offset the harmful effects of radishes, eat leeks; to offset the harmful effects of leeks, drink hot water. Hot water nullifies the harmful effects of all vegetables.

31. After every food eat salt, and after every beverage drink water, and you will not come to harm.

32. Who dies in the midst of laughter it is a good omen for him, but amidst weeping it is a bad omen for him.

33. The eye which does not desire that which belongs to others cannot be influenced by the Evil Eye.

34. The male hyena after seven years becomes a bat; the bat after seven years becomes a vampire; the vampire after seven years becomes a nettle; the nettle after seven years becomes a thorn; the thorn after seven years bcomes a demon.

35. To cure a tertian fever: take seven prickles from seven palm trees, seven chips from seven beams, seven nails from seven bridges, seven ashes from seven ovens, seven particles of dust from seven door sockets, seven pieces of pitch from seven ships, seven handfuls of cumin, and seven hairs from the beard of an old dog, and tie them to the neck of the shirt with a white twisted cord.

36. The sun is red in the morning and evening: in the morning because it passes over (and catches the reflection of) the roses of the Garden of Eden, and in the evening because it passes over the entrance of *Gehinnom*.

37. The world is a sixtieth part of the Garden of Eden; the Garden of Eden is a sixtieth part of *Gehinnom*.

38. One born on a Sunday will be wholly good or wholly bad, because on that day light and darkness were created;
    One born on Monday will be bad-tempered, because on that day the waters were divided;
    One born on Tuesday will be rich and lustful, because on that day the herbs and fruits were created;
    One born on Wednesday will be wise and of retentive

memory, because on that day the luminaries were suspended in the firmament;

One born on Thursday will be benevolent, because on that day fish and birds were created;

One born on Friday will be active, or according to another version, zealous to perform the precepts;

One born on the Sabbath will die on the Sabbath, because on his account the holy day was profaned.

39. Friday is an unlucky day: Adam sinned on Friday and was expelled from the Garden of Eden; thistles and thorns and poisonous plants began to grow on that day, after the expulsion of Adam and Eve; Cain killed his brother Abel on a Friday; and Moses died on a Friday.

40. Tuesday is an especially lucky day, for on the first Tuesday God saw what he did and *twice* said that it was "good."

41. One born under the influence of the sun will be a distinguished man; will eat and drink of his own, his secrets will be revealed, and if he should venture to steal he will not succeed;

One born under the influence of Venus will be rich and lustful, because fire was born through that constellation;

One born under the influence of Mercury will be of retentive memory and wise, because it is the scribe of (i.e., attendent upon) the sun;

One born under the influence of the moon will be ailing, will build and destroy and again destroy and build; will eat and drink not of his own, his secrets will be concealed, and if he should venture to steal he will succeed;

One born under the influence of Saturn will be a man whose plans will fail, but others declare that all designs against him will fail;

One born under the influence of Jupiter will be righteous;

One born under the influence of Mars will be a shedder of blood. (He will be either a cupper, a butcher, or a circumciser.)

42. To dream of liquids other than wine is a bad omen.

43. He who dreams of a well will see peace.

44. An uninterpreted dream is like an unread letter.

45. Dreams are a sixtieth part of prophecy.

46. Neither a good nor a bad dream is fulfilled in every detail.

47. A bad dream is preferable to a good dream! When a dream is bad, the pain it causes is sufficient to prevent its fulfillment; when a dream is good, the joy it brings is sufficient.

48. A good man does not necessarily have a good dream; and a bad man does not necessarily have a bad dream.

49. There are three dreams which fortell peace: a river, a bird, and a pot.

50. Who dreams of wheat will see peace.

Who dreams of olives, his business will be fruitful and endure.

Who dreams of a well-laden vine, his wife will not miscarry.

Who dreams of a goat, the year will be blessed for him.

Who dreams of pomegranates, his business will bear fruit.

Who dreams of the myrtle, his business undertakings will prosper.

Who dreams of a citron will be honored before his Maker.

Who dreams of a goose, may hope for wisdom.

Who dreams of a cock, may hope for a son.

Who dreams of eggs, his petition remains in suspense.

Who dreams that he entered a town, his desires will be fulfilled.

Who dreams of ascending to the roof will ascend to greatness.

KEY TO SOURCE BOOKS FOR THE PRECEPTS, PROVERBS, AND FOLK BELIEFS

Key to Symbols:

ARN *Abot d'Rabbi Natan* (*The Sayings of the Fathers* according to Rabbi Nathan), in Hebrew, edited by S. Z. Schechter.

ET *Everyman's Talmud,* in English, by A. Cohen. This secondary source is given because of its greater availability to most readers.

MR *Midrash Rabah* (The Great Midrashim on the Five Books of Moses and the Five Megilot: Song of Songs, Ruth, Lamentations, Ecclesiastes, and Esther). This great and voluminous work has been translated into English by Maurice Simon and edited by H. Freedman, and has been issued in ten volumes by the Soncino Press in London.

PA *Pirke Abot* (Sayings of the Fathers), in Hebrew; the Ninth Tractate in the Order *Nezikin* (Torts) in the Mishna. Available in many English translations. (*See* SF)

SF *Sayings of the Fathers* (*See* PA), in English, with parallel text in Hebrew, by Dr. Joseph H. Hertz, late Chief Rabbi of the British Empire, with excellent commentaries.

T *The Talmud* (The Study of the Mishna), in Hebrew and Aramaic. There are two, and differing, versions of the Talmud: the Babylonian and the Palestinian. All precepts and proverbs given in this book are from the Babylonian Talmud, which is now available in English, edited by Isidore Epstein and published by Soncino Press in London.

PRECEPTS

1. Hasidic Folk Saying
2. PA (SF): II, 6
3. PA (SF): I, 15
4. PA (SF): I, 1
5. PA (SF): IV, 24
6. PA (SF): IV, 27
7. ARN: XLI
8. PA (SF): I, 4
9. PA (SF): I, 6
10. PA (SF): I, 8
11. PA (SF): II, 5
12. PA (SF): II, 5
13. PA (SF): II, 17
14. PA (SF): III, 16
15. SF III, Note on 6, p. 50
16. T: Sotah 32b
17. PA (SF): I, 10
18. PA (SF): II, 15

19. PA (SF): II, 18
20. PA (SF): III, 2
21. PA (SF): II, 3
22. PA (SF): IV, 7
23. PA (SF): IV, 13
24. PA (SF): IV, 23
25. PA (SF): IV, 16
26. SF: p. 127
27. PA (SF): I, 1
28. PA (SF): I, 9
29. PA (SF): IV, 10
30. ET: 307
31. ET: 308
32. MR: Num.: XXXV, 30
33. ET: 309
34. T: Sanhedrin, 49a
35. PA (SF): II, 16
36. T: Gittin, V, 8

37. PA (SF): III, 18
38. ET: 177
39. ARN: XII
40. T: Taanit, 20b
41. T: Baba Kamma, 92a
42. T: Yebamot, 105b
43. ET: 82
44. ET: 81
45. T: Sukkah, 46b
46. Sefer Hasidim, p. 126
47. Hasidic Folk Saying
48. Pesikta Zutarti Behaalot'ha
49. Berahot, 17
50. Sanhedrin, 71

PROVERBS

Faith and Prayer

1. T: Megillah, 13a
2. ARN: XXXI
3. MR: Deut.: II, 12
4. ET: 385

5. Hasidic Folk Saying
6. MR: Exod.: XXI, 3
7. T: Hagigah, 5b
8. T: Berahot, 33b

9. ET: 237
10. T: Berahot, 24b
11. ET: 22
12. T: Megillah, 13a
13. MR: Gen. LI

Truth and Falsehood

14. T: Shabbat, 104a
15. T: Shabbat, 104a
16. Hasidic Folk Saying

17. ET: 15
18. Hasidic Folk Saying
19. T: Sanhedrin, 89b

20. Hasidic Folk Saying
21. PA (SF): I, 18

Justice and Peace

22. T: Hagigah, 12b
23. ET: 208
24. T: Sanhedrin, 7a
25. PA (SF): V, 11
26. ET: 209

27. T: Sanhedrin, 7b
28. T: Behorot, LV, 6
29. T: Shebuot, 31a
30. ET: 190

31. T: Taanit, 7a
32. T: Behorot, IV, 6
33. ET: 23
34. ET: 209

Wisdom and Folly

35. Yiddish Proverb
36. PA (SF): IV, 1
37. PA (SF): V, 10
38. Hasidic Folk Saying
39. PA (SF): IV, 20
40. T: Ketubot, 5b
41. Hasidic Folk Saying

42. MR: Leviticus
43. PA (SF): III, 17
44. Yiddish Proverb
45. T: Pesahim, 99a
46. PA (SF): III, 22
47. PA (SF): III, 12
48. SF, 128
49. ET: 88
50. T: Pesahim, 66b
51. PA (SF): I, 14

52. Hasidic Folk Saying
53. PA (SF): II, 6
54. T: Megillah, 182
55. Hasidic Folk Saying
56. Hasidic Folk Saying
57. Esdras II: IV, 26

Virtue and Sin

58. T: Avodah Zarah, 20b
59. PA (SF): I, 17
60. T: Sanhedrin, 7a
61. ARN: XXIII
62. Sanhedrin, 88b
63. T: Sukkah, 49b
64. T: Gittin, 7b
65. T: Baba Batra, 9a
66. T: Baba Batra, 10b
67. PA (SF): I, 13
68. ARN: XIII
69. ET: 222
70. T: Ketubot, 66b
71. ET: 368
72. Hasidic Folk Saying

73. PA (SF): I, 16
74. T: Sotah, IX, 15
75. T: Shabbat, 55a
76. T: Yoma, 86a
77. ET: 108
78. Sotah, 32
79. ET: 95
80. PA (SF): III, 19
81. MR: Gen. XXXIV, 10
82. T: Sukkah, 52b
83. T: Sukkah, 52a
84. T: Sukkah, 52a
85. T: Shabbat, 14
86. ET: 18
87. T: Berahot, 61a
88. ARN: XVI
89. T: Arahin, 30a

90. T: Sanhedrin, 19b
91. T: Arahin, 15b
92. T: Arahin, 15b
93. T: Yoma, 43a
94. PA (SF): II, 1
95. PA (SF): IV, 19
96. PA (SF): III, 17
97. PA (SF): IV, 2
98. T: Yoma, 86b
99. T: Berahot, IX, 5
100. T: Sotah, 32
101. T: Taanit, 8b
102. PA (SF): V, 22
103. T: Erubin, 100b
104. PA (SF): IV, 28
105. ET: 103

106. T: Berahot, 12b
107. PA (SF): IV, 22
108. T: Berahot, 34
109. MR: Lev. XXIII, 12
110. ET: 96
111. T: Yoma, 9b
112. T: Berahot, 55a
113. T: Yoma, 86b

114. T: Sotah, 16
115. ET: 206
116. T: Berahot, 29b
117. ET: 232
118. T: Pesahim, 113b
119. PA (SF): V, 14
120. T: Nedarim, 39b

121. T: Sotah, 31a
122. PA (SF): V, 13
123. PA (SF): IV, 17
124. T: Berahot, 34
125. MR: Lev., XXXIV, 8
126. ET: 221
127. ET: 206
128. T: Shabbat, II, 5

Poverty and Riches

129. ET: 230
130. PA (SF): III, 21
131. T: Betzah, 32b
132. T: Baba Metzia, 38a

133. Hasidic Folk Saying
134. T: Shabbat, 152a
135. ET: 234
136. T: Shabbat, 25b

137. Hasidic Folk Saying
138. PA (SF): II, 8
139. T: Shabbat, 32a

Knowledge and Ignorance

140. PA (SF): II, 8
141. MR: Lev., I, 6
142. Hasidic Folk Saying
143. PA (SF): I, 2
144. PA (SF): I, 13
145. PA (SF): III, 21
146. ET: 139
147. T: Sanhedrin, 19b
148. PA (SF): IV, 25
149. T: Rosh Hashanah, 23a

150. PA (SF): II, 6
151. PA (SF): II, 6
152. PA (SF): II, 6
153. PA (SF): I, 17
154. PA (SF): II, 2
155. T: Nedarim, 62a
156. T: Nedarim, 81a
157. T: Shabbat, 119b
158. PA (SF): III, 21

159. T: Kiddushin, 40b
160. Hasidic Folk Saying
161. T: Hagigah, 5b
162. PA (SF): IV, 26
163. T: Pesahim, 3b
164. T: Erubin, 54b
165. T: Baba Batra, 21a
166. T: Gittin, 58a
167. PA (SF): V, 15
168. PA (SF): V, 18

Women

169. T: Mo'ed Katan, 9b

170. T: Megillah, 14b

171. T: Megillah, 14b

172. T: Shabbat,
    33b
173. T: Kiddushin,
    49b
174. T: Berahot,
    61a
175. T: Berahot,
    61a

176. T: Ketubot,
    65a
177. PA (SF): V, 10
178. Hasidic Folk
    Saying
179. T: Ketubot,
    65a

180. T: Ketubot,
    30a
181. T: Megillah,
    14b
182. T: Yoma, 66b
183. PA (SF): I, 5
184. T: Niddah, 45b

Marriage and Divorce

185. T: Baba
    Metzia, 59a
186. T: Sanhedrin,
    22a
187. T: Baba
    Metzia, 59a
188. T: Yebamot,
    62b
189. T: Yoma, I, 1
190. T: Yebamot,
    63a

191. T: Yebamot,
    101b
192. T: Megillah,
    27a
193. T: Kiddushin,
    70a
194. T: Behorot,
    45b
195. T: Pesahim,
    49a
196. Hasidic Folk
    Saying

197. T: Sotah, 3b
198. T: Yebamot,
    63b
199. T: Gittin, IX,
    10
200. T: Ketubot,
    III, 5
201. T: Ketubot,
    77a
202. T: Hullin, 846

Parents and Children

203. T: Shabbat,
    10b
204. T: Kiddushin,
    41a
205. T: Sanhedrin,
    100b

206. T: Kiddushin,
    31a
207. T: Baba Batra,
    16b
208. MR: Gen.,
    LXXI, 6

209. TZ: I, 186
210. T: Gittin, 6b
211. ET: 172
212. ET: 172
213. ET: 172

The Community

214. MR: Lev.,
    IV, 6
215. ET: 188
216. PA (SF): II, 5

217. T: Taanit, 23a
218. T: Sanhedrin,
    22a

219. T: Baba
    Metzia, 86b
220. T: Baba
    Metzia, 86b

War and Peace

221. MR: Genesis

222. PA (SF): I, 18

223. ARN: XXXVII

224. ET: 204
225. MR: Deut.,
5:14
226. PA (SF): I, 12
227. MR: Lev.,
XIX, 18

228. T: Sanhedrin,
IV, 5
229. Hasidic Folk
Saying

230. Hasidic Folk
Saying
231. Hasidic Folk
Saying

Work and the Worker

232. T: Pesahim,
113a
233. ET: 195
234. T: Sanhedrin,
29a
235. ET: 195
236. T: Nedarim,
49b

237. ARN: XI
238. ET: 193
239. PA (SF): II, 21
240. PA (SF): V, 6
241. MR: Gen.,
XIV, 10
242. T: Ketubot,
V, 5
243. FJ: 146

244. ET: 195
245. ET: 197
246. T: Baba
Metzia, 86b
247. T: Baba
Metzia, 71a
248. T: Berahot,
40a

Health and Cleanliness

249. T: Berahot,
62b
250. Hasidic Folk
Saying
251. T: Sanhedrin,
17b
252. T: Baba
Kamma, 85a
253. T: Shabbat,
50b
254. T: Kiddushin,
66b
255. T: Shabbat,
41a

256. Hasidic Folk
Saying
257. T: Berahot,
37b
258. T: Avodah
Zarah, 20b
259. T: Erubin, 65a
260. T: Ketubot,
111a
261. T: Gittin, 70a
262. T: Sukkah,
26b
263. ET: 246
264. T: Gittin, 70a

265. T: Shabbat,
108b
266. T: Yoma, 78b
267. ET: 241
268. T: Sotah, 4b
269. T: Sotah, 4b
270. T: Berahot,
25a
271. T: Sanhedrin,
17b
272. T: Berahot, 58b
273. ET: 243
274. ET: 121, 239

Food and Medicine

275. T: Baba
Kamma, 92b
276. T: Yoma, 63a
277. T: Baba
Kamma, 58b

278. T: Gittin, 70a
279. T: Berahot,
62b
280. T: Shabbat,
158a

281. T: Pesahim,
113a
282. T: Sanhedrin,
70a
283. T: Taanit, 10b

284. T: Shebuot, 15b
285. MR: Num., X, 8
286. T: Sanhedrin, 70
287. T: Berahot, 40a
288. T: Ketubot, 10b
289. T: Berahot, 40a
290. ET: 247
291. TZ: II, 368
292. T: Berahot, 60a
293. T: Baba Batra, 12b

Death and the Life Hereafter

294. MR: Gen., XCVI, 2
295. Hasidic Folk Saying
296. MR: Gen., 9; Exod., XXVI, 2
297. PA (SF): IV, 21
298. T: Shabbat, 31a
299. ET: 381
300. PA (SF): II, 20

FOLK BELIEFS

1. T: Baba Batra, 141a
2. T: Berahot, 55b
3. ET: 282
4. T: Horayot, 13b
5. T: Baba Metzia, 107b
6. T: Mo'ed Katan, 28a
7. ET: 262
8. T: Yebamot, 15
9. ET: 270
10. T: Berahot, 24b
11. T: Rosh Hashanah, 16b
12. T: Berahot, 20a
13. ET: 273
14. T: Berahot, 7b
15. T: Shabbat, 8
16. T: Berahot, 55b
17. T: Baba Kamma, 93a
18. T: Horayot, 13b
19. T: Horayot, 13b
20. T: Baba Kamma, 85a
21. T: Erubin, 56a
22. T: Baba Kamma, 82a
23. T: Shabbat, 108b
24. T: Niddah, 17a
25. T: Berahot, 44b
26. T: Berahot, 44b
27. T: Berahot, 44b
28. T: Berahot, 40a
29. T: Berahot, 40a
30. T: Pesahim, 116a
31. T. Berahot, 40a
32. T: Ketubot, 103b
33. T: Berahot, 20a
34. T: Baba Kamma, 16a
35. T: Shabbat, 66b
36. T: Baba Batra, 84a
37. T: Taanit, 10a
38. T: Shabbat, 156a
39. FJ: 62
40. FJ: 62
41. T: Shabbat, 156a
42. T: Berahot, 57a
43. T: Berahot, 55a
44. T: Berahot, 55a
45. T: Berahot, 57b
46. T: Berahot, 55a
47. T: Berahot, 55a
48. ET: 287
49. T: Berahot, 55b
50. ET: 290-1

PART VII

THE JEWISH BOOKSHELF

"Study leads to practice"
—Talmud Kiddushin, 406

ACCORDING TO LEGEND, it was Mohammed who described the Jews as "The People of the Book," and the Jews accepted the description as a badge of honor. For many generations Jews have become proverbial among the nations for their love of learning.

Every Jew, young or old, strong or feeble, is obliged to study the Torah—and this term, which at first designated the Five Books of Moses, was gradually broadened to include all the books that extend man's vision and enlarge his understanding of God's universe. It was incumbent on all the Children of Israel to devote some time each day to the study of the Book or books. "Even a poor man living on charity or going about seeking alms," said Maimonides, the great medieval Jewish teacher, "must set apart a period, day and night, for the study of the Torah. For whenever he fails to devote himself to study, he is certain to forget."

A Jewish home without any books is inconceivable. And among the books most likely to be found in the American Jewish home that honors the Jewish heritage are those that relate to this heritage: the Bible and books about the Bible; prayer books and books on Jewish holidays and customs; selections from the Talmud and descriptions of its contents; books on Jewish history, on the Jewish liturgy, on Jewish music, art, philosophy, humor, and so on. And, of course, general works of fiction, drama, and poetry dealing with Jewish life, past and present.

Jawaharlal Nehru made the profound observation that it is hard to keep the idea of freedom from people who habitually read. The communication of the written word enlarges knowledge, it broadens understanding, and it nurtures a love of freedom. The traditional love of learning has imbued Jews with a love of freedom. And the place of honor that the bookshelf has in the Jewish home reflects the householder's democratic ideals as much as the *mezuzah* upon the post of his door symbolizes his belonging to the Judaic faith.

Here is a brief list of books that ought to be found in every Jewish home. The limitation is avowedly arbitrary, but it is a good starting point. The titles recommended are primarily for adults and subjectively chosen. If there are children in the home, other books can be found on most of the topics included and at all age levels. But the adult books are the foundation of the Jewish home library.

For most of the books recommended here there are some (and in some instances many) alternate or equivalent versions: the choice will reflect the taste of the chooser—and tastes differ. The following books are therefore highly recommended with the warning that they reflect the authors' inclinations, and each person acquiring a library will have to substitute his or her own inclinations when buying books.

The Jewish library begins with the Bible.

THE BIBLE

There ought to be at least two Bibles in every Jewish home; and three, if any member of the family can read Hebrew. For those who can read it in the original Hebrew, there can be no substitute. Every language has its own idiom, its own atmosphere, its own sweetness; and no translation, however excellent, can communicate these qualities fully. Then there ought to be one Bible in English for traditional and liturgical use and another for inspirational reading. The two are not the same. In addition, every home should have at least one good book *about* the Bible, its origins, its growth, its canonization, its varied books, and how to read them probingly. There are many versions available to choose from in all three categories. Here are three we recommend:

1. *The Holy Scriptures* (in Hebrew). The accurate Masoretic text of the Hebrew Bible, edited by the Hebrew writer and scholar Meir Halevi Letteris, has been printed in clear, legible type by the British and Foreign Bible Society. It is readily available in inexpensive editions. Other excellent editions of the Hebrew text have been published in Israel by the Hebrew University, and in the United States by the Jewish Publication Society, the latter with the Society's English translation.

2. *The Holy Scriptures* (in English). Published by the Jewish Publication Society of America, Philadelphia, 1917. Jews do not have an English version officially sanctioned by the synagogue, comparable to the Authorized Version for some Protestant Churches, or the Revised Standard Version for others, or the Douay Version for the Roman Catholic Church. However, the Jewish Publication Society (J.P.S.) edition has found general acceptance for use in worship, in synagogue and home.

3. *The Jewish Bible for Family Reading,* a new version by Joseph Gaer (Thomas Yoseloff, Inc., N.Y., 1957). This is the complete Holy Scriptures from which all genealogies, duplications, and archaisms have been eliminated, and so arranged that it can be read by every member of the family with ease and enjoyment. The general introduction, "The Bible: Our Inheritance," makes clear how the Bible grew and how it should be read today. Twenty-six brief introductions guide the reader through the Books of the Bible; they are supplemented with a digest of the Apocrypha and a Summary of the principal laws in the Pentateuch, alphabetically arranged.

THE PRAYERBOOK

The Prayerbook in the Jewish home reflects the religious thoughts and habits of its occupants. There are many good editions of the traditional Prayerbooks for Sabbath and weekday, and for the various holidays, the *Siddur* and the *Mahzor*. Some of these editions reflect the regional differences between Jews from various countries (see pp. 20-22). One of the best editions of the Prayerbook for Sabbath and weekdays, acceptable in most Orthodox congregations in America, printed with English translation and commentary, is *The Authorized Daily Prayer Book*, edited by Dr. Joseph H. Hertz (Bloch Publishing Company, New York, 1948). For New Year and the Day of Atonement, there is *Service of the Synagogue: New Year and Day of Atonement*, edited by Naphtali Adler and Jacob Davis (Hebrew Publishing Company, New York), and, for Passover, Feast of Weeks, and Tabernacles, *Festival Services for Passover, Feast of Weeks and Tabernacles*, edited by H. M. Adler and several others (Hebrew Publishing Company).

The Conservative movement has published its official *Sabbath and Festival Prayer Book* (New York, 1946), with English translation, supplementary readings, and notes. For the High Holidays most Conservative congregations use *High Holiday Prayer Book*, edited and translated by Rabbi Morris Silverman (Hartford, Connecticut).

For the Reform Jewish home, four volumes of prayers have been published under the imprint of the Central Conference of American Rabbis. *The Union Prayerbook for Jewish Worship*, Part I (Newly Revised, Cincinnati, 1940) contains prayers for Sabbath, weekdays, and the festivals. *The Union Prayerbook for Jewish Worship*, Part II (Newly Revised, Cincinnati, 1945), is devoted to New Year and the Day of Atonement. *The Union Home Prayerbook* (Philadelphia, 1951) contains prayers for family worship and personal prayers for special occasions. The *Union Haggadah* (copyright, 1923) presents and explains the home service for the Passover.

THE LITERATURE OF THE TALMUD

The Talmud is a literary world all of its own. No Jewish library is complete without the impressive shelf of folio volumes which form the basis of Jewish religious law. The most famous edition is that published in Vilna, in 1922. Relatively inexpensive photostatically reproduced editions in smaller size are also available of the Babylonian Talmud, of the Palestinian Talmud, as well as the Midrash Rabba. To the serious student who does not read Hebrew and talmudic Aramaic, English translations are available of both the Talmud and the Midrash, published by the Soncino Press in London. (The Babylonian Talmud, 34 volumes, 1948; The Midrash Rabba, 10 volumes, 1939.) Even in English translation these volumes remain difficult reading; and the average reader will prefer the excerpts and popularizations recommended on the following pages.

BOOKS ON JEWISH LIFE AND LETTERS

The Bible

1. *Preface to Scripture,* by Solomon B. Freehof. Union of American Hebrew Congregations, 1950.
2. *Companion to the Bible,* by Abraham J. Feldman. Little, Brown and Company, 1952.

Biblical Lore

3. *The Legends of the Jews,* by Louis Ginzberg. Jewish Publication Society of America, 1910-1938 (New Edition, 1954). (A scholarly and exhaustive collection; copious notes.)
4. *The Lore of the Old Testament,* by Joseph Gaer. Little, Brown and Company, Boston, 1951. (Over three hundred legends, from diverse sources, chronologically arranged, which present the Bible as it appears in folk imagination.)

The Talmud

5. *Everyman's Talmud,* by A. Cohen. New American edition. E. P. Dutton & Co., New York, 1949. (A comprehensive summary of the teachings of the Talmud.)

6. *The Wisdom of the Talmud,* by Ben Zion Bokser. Philosophical Library, New York.

Philosophy

7. *A History of Jewish Medieval Philosophy,* by Isaac Husik. The Macmillan Co., New York, 1918. (A scholarly appraisal of the medieval Jewish philosophers.)

8. *Modern Philosophies of Judaism,* by Jacob B. Agus. Behrman House, Inc., New York, 1941. (Supplements and brings up to date Isaac Husik's work above.)

Literature

9. *The Wisdom of Israel,* by Lewis Browne. Random House, New York, 1945. (An excellent introduction to Jewish literature.)

10. *The Jewish Caravan,* by Leo W. Schwarz. Farrar & Rinehart, New York, 1935. (Great stories of twenty-five centuries.)

11. *A History of Jewish Literature,* by Meyer Waxman, Ph.D. Bloch Publishing Co., Inc., New York, 1936, 4 volumes.

12. *Jewish Literature Since the Bible,* by Leon I. Feuer. Union of American Hebrew Congregations, Cincinnati, 1942, 2 volumes.

13. *The Great Jewish Books,* by Samuel Caplan. Horizon Press, Inc., New York, 1952.

Liturgy

14. *The Small Sanctuary,* by Solomon B. Freehof. Union of American Hebrew Congregations, Cincinnati, 1942. (Gives a clear explanation of Jewish experience in worship and a description of the liturgy as practiced today.)

15. *Jewish Ideals and Values in the Prayer Book,* by Dr. Simon Greenberg. United Synagogue of America, New York, n.d.

Religion and Religious Movements

16. *Judaism, A Way of Life,* by Samuel S. Cohen. Union of American Hebrew Congregations, Cincinnati, 1948. (A comprehensive study of Jewish beliefs, ideals, ethics, and religious practice.)

17. *Judaism as Creed and Life,* by Morris Joseph. Routledge & Son, London, 1925. (A popular presentation of the principles and ideals of Jewish faith and conduct.)

18. *Jewish Theology,* by Kaufman Kohler. The Macmillan Co., New York, 1928. (A systematic exposition of the Jewish faith from the viewpoint of historical research.)

19. *Man's Quest for God,* by Abraham Joshua Heschel. Charles Scribner's Sons, New York, 1954. (An inquiry into the nature of man's relationship with God through the study of Jewish prayer and symbolism.)

20. *The Jewish Religion,* by M. Friedlænder. Vallentine & Son, London, 1913. (The nature of Judaism and its ceremonials, from the Orthodox point of view.)

21. *The Reform Movement in Judaism,* by David Philipson. The Macmillan Co., New York, 1931. (A detailed account of the political, cultural, and religious factors which gave impetus to the Reform movement and an analysis of its ideas and activities.)

22. *The Future of the American Jew,* by Mordecai M. Kaplan. The Macmillan Co., New York, 1948. (A plan for the reorganization of American Jewry and a pattern for tomorrow's Judaism from the Reconstructionist point of view, by the founder and elder statesman of the Reconstructionist movement.)

Jewish History

23. *A Bird's-Eye View of Jewish History,* by C. Roth. Union of American Hebrew Congregations, Cincinnati, 1935. (A condensation of thirty centuries of Jewish history.)

24. *A History of the Jews,* by Abram Leon Sachar. Alfred A. Knopf, New York, 1940. (A scholarly one-volume history of the Jews brought up to date.)

25. *The Jews: Their History, Culture and Religion,* by Louis Finkelstein, Editor. Jewish Publication Society of America, Philadelphia, 1949, 2 volumes.

Contributions to Civilization

26. *The Legacy of Israel,* ed. by Edwyn R. Bevan and Charles Singer. Clarendon Press, Oxford, 1927. (Particularly valuable for its study of the debt of Christianity to Judaism, and of the influence of Judaism on Western law.)

27. *Jewish Contributions to Civilization,* by Joseph Jacobs. Jewish

Publication Society of America, Philadelphia, 1919. (A serious, if incomplete, study by a distinguished scholar.)

28. *The Hebrew Impact on Western Civilization,* edited by Dagobert D. Runes. Philosophical Library, New York, 1951. (Jewish contributions in all fields of knowledge.)

Israel

29. *Israel Without Tears,* by Ruth Gruber. A. A. Wyn, Inc., New York, 1950. (A humorous book on the new state.)

30. *Israel; The Beginning and Tomorrow,* by Harold A. Lehrman. William Sloane, New York, 1952. (A reporter's bird's-eye view of the Israeli state and its future.)

31. *Trial and Error,* by Chaim Weizman. Harper & Brothers, New York, 1949. (The great autobiography of the first President of Israel.)

Jews in the United States

32. *Jewish Pioneers and Patriots,* by Lee M. Friedman. The Macmillan Co., New York, 1943. (A study of Jewish participation in the building of America.)

33. *The American Jew,* by Oscar I. Janowsky. Harper & Brothers, New York, 1942.

34. *History of the Jews in the U. S.,* by Joseph Lee Levinger. Union of American Hebrew Congregations, Cincinnati, 1935.

35. *Early American Jewry,* by Jacob R. Marcus. Jewish Publication Society, Philadelphia, 1951 and 1953, 2 volumes.

Holidays and Ceremonials

36. *Jewish Holidays and Festivals,* by Ben M. Edidin. Hebrew Publishing Co., New York, 1940. (Gives an adequate description of each of the Jewish holidays.)

37. *The Jewish Festivals,* by Hayyim Schauss, translated by Samuel Jaff. Union of American Hebrew Congregations, Cincinnati, 1938.

38. *The Lifetime of a Jew,* by Hayyim Schauss. Union of American Hebrew Congregations, Cincinnati, 1950.

Mysticism

39. *The Zohar,* translated by Harry Sterling and Maurice Simon. Soncino Press, London, 1931-34, 5 volumes. (For those who wish to explore this great source of Jewish mysticism in five long volumes.)

40. *The Hasidic Anthology,* by Louis I. Newman. Charles Scribner's Sons, New York, 1934. (An immense collection, organized topically.)

41. *The Earth Is the Lord's,* by Abraham Heschel. Schuman Co., New York, 1950. (A summation of the spirit of Jewish mysticism as it appears in the Hasidic movement.)

The Arts

42. *A Short History of Jewish Art,* by Helen Rosenbau. J. Clarke, London, 1948. (Might serve as a starting point for the reader to whom this field is new.)

43. *A History of Jewish Art,* by Franz Landsberger. Union of American Hebrew Congregations, Cincinnati, 1946. (Informative and contains a good bibliography.)

44. *Hebrew Music,* by David Ewen. Bloch Publishing Co., Inc., New York, 1941. (The best general survey of this topic.)

45. *A Treasury of Jewish Folksong,* by Ruth Rubin. Schocken Books, Inc., New York, 1950. (A good selection, well presented by a music editor.)

Humor

46. *A Treasury of Jewish Humor,* by Nathan Ausubel. Doubleday & Company, Inc., New York, 1951.

General

47. *What is a Jew?* by Rabbi Morris N. Kertzer. World Publishing Co., New York, 1953. (A delightful book that gives concise answers to 100 questions concerning various aspects of Judaism in our times.)

48. *Basic Judaism,* by Milton Steinberg. Harcourt, Brace & Co., New York, 1947. (A perceptive book, written with insight and lucidity by the late Rabbi Steinberg, who gave us also *As a Driven Leaf,* a novel of talmudic times; and *A Believing Jew,* a group of 23 thought-provoking essays.)

PART VIII

SELECTIONS FROM
THE DAILY PRAYERS

"All are equal before God in prayer."
—Midrash Rabah, Ex. 21

THE MORNING SERVICE (*SHAHARIT*)

(The entire service is found in *O-1*, pp. 4-271; *R-1*, pp. 311-71.)

Eloha'i N'shamah

Happy are they who dwell in Thy house, they are continually praising Thee. Incline Thine ear and answer us, be gracious unto us, O God, and cause us to rejoice, for unto Thee we lift up our souls. Teach us Thy way that we may walk firmly in Thy truth. Show us Thy kindness, grant us Thy salvation. Be with us this day and at all times, O Thou, our God and our Father, our Rock and our Redeemer.

The soul which Thou, O God, hast given unto me came pure from Thee. Thou hast created it, Thou hast formed it, Thou hast breathed it into me; Thou hast preserved it in this body; and, at the appointed time, Thou wilt take it from this earth that it may enter upon life everlasting. While the breath of life is within me I will worship Thee, Sovereign of the world and Lord of all souls. Praised be Thou, O God, in whose hands are the souls of all the living and the spirits of all flesh. (*R-1*, p. 312; cf. *O-1*, p. 19)

Viy'hi Ratson

And may it be thy will, O Lord our God and God of our fathers, to accustom us to walk in thy Torah, and to make us cleave to thy commandments. O lead us not into sin, or transgression, iniquity, temptation, or disgrace: let not the evil inclination have sway over us: keep us far from a bad man and a bad companion: make us cleave to the good inclination and to good works: subdue our inclination so that it may submit itself to thee: and let us obtain this day, and every day, grace, favour, and mercy in thine eyes, and in the eyes of all who behold us; and

195

bestow lovingkindnesses upon us. Blessed art thou, O Lord, who bestowest lovingkindnesses upon thy people Israel. (*O-1*, p. 25)

Ribon

Lord of all worlds, not in reliance upon our own merit do we lay our supplications before Thee, but trusting in Thine infinite mercy alone. For what are we, what is our life, what our goodness, what our power? What can we say in Thy presence? Are not all the mighty men as naught before Thee and those of great renown as though they had never been; the wisest as if without knowledge, and men of understanding as if without discernment? Many of our works are vain, and our days pass away like a shadow. Our life would be altogether vanity, were it not for the soul which, fashioned in Thine own image, gives us assurance of our higher destiny and imparts to our fleeting days an abiding value. (*R-1*, p. 101; cf. *O-1*, pp. 27-29)

Bar'hu

Bless ye the Lord who is to be blessed.

Blessed is the Lord who is to be blessed for ever and ever.

Blessed art thou, O Lord our God, King of the universe, who formest light and createst darkness, who makest peace and createst all things:

Who in mercy givest light to the earth and to them that dwell thereon, and in thy goodness renewest the creation every day continually. How manifold are thy works, O Lord! In wisdom hast thou made them all: the earth is full of thy creatures. O King, who alone wast exalted from aforetime, praised, glorified and extolled from days of old; O everlasting God, in thine abundant mercies, have mercy upon us, Lord of our strength, Rock of our stronghold, Shield of our salvation, thou Stronghold of ours! (*O-1*, pp. 109-11; cf. *R-1*, p. 314)

Sh'ma

Hear, O Israel: the Lord is our God, the Lord is One.

Blessed be His name, whose glorious kingdom is for ever and ever.

And thou shalt love the Lord thy God with all thine heart, and with all thy soul, and with all thy might. And these words, which I command thee this day, shall be upon thine heart: and thou shalt teach them diligently unto thy children, and shalt talk of them when thou sittest in thine house, and when thou walkest by the way, and when thou liest down, and when thou risest up. And thou shalt bind them for a sign upon thine hand, and they shall be for frontlets between thine eyes. And thou shalt write them upon the door-posts of thy house, and upon thy gates. (*O-1*, pp. 117-19; cf. *R-1*, p. 316)

T'filah

Nos. 1, 2. Blessed art thou, O Lord our God and God of our fathers, God of Abraham, God of Isaac, and God of Jacob, the great, mighty and revered God, the most high God, who bestowest lovingkindnesses, and art Master of all things; who rememberest the pious deeds of the patriarchs, and in love wilt bring a redeemer to their children's children for thy Name's sake.

(*During the Ten Days of Repentance say*: Remember us unto life, O king, who delightest in life, and inscribe us in the book of life, for thine own sake, O living God.)

O King, Helper, Saviour and Shield. Blessed art thou, O Lord, the Shield of Abraham.

Thou, O Lord, art mighty for ever, thou revivest the dead, thou art mighty to save. (*O-1*, pp. 131-34; cf. *R-1*, pp. 320-21)

No. 16. Hear our voice, O Lord our God; spare us and have mercy upon us, and accept our prayer in mercy and favour; for thou art a God who hearkenest unto prayers and supplications: from thy presence, O our King, turn us not empty away; for thou hearkenest in mercy to the prayer of thy people Israel. Blessed art thou, O Lord, who hearkenest unto prayer. (*O-1*, p. 147; cf. *R-1*, p. 322)

No. 18. We gratefully acknowledge, O Lord, our God, that Thou art our Creator and Preserver, the Rock of our life and the Shield of our help. We render thanks unto Thee for our lives which are in Thy hand, for our souls which are ever in Thy keeping; for Thy wondrous providence and for Thy continuous goodness, which Thou bestowest upon us day by day. Truly, Thy

mercies never fail and Thy lovingkindness never ceases. Therefore do we forever put our trust in Thee. (*R-1*, p. 324; cf. *O-1*,
p. 151)

No. 19. Grant us peace, Thy most precious gift, O Thou eternal source of peace, and enable Israel to be its messenger unto
the peoples of the earth. Bless our country that it may ever be a
stronghold of peace, and its advocate in the council of nations.
May contentment reign within its borders, health and happiness
within its homes. Strengthen the bonds of friendship and fellowship among all the inhabitants of our land. Plant virtue in every
soul, and may the love of Thy name hallow every home and
every heart. Praise be Thou, O Lord, Giver of peace. (*R-1*, p.
324; cf. *O-1*, p. 155)

Short form of Amidah

Heavenly Father, who hast graciously endowed mankind with
reason and understanding, send us the light of Thy truth, that
we may gain insight into the wisdom of Thy ways. Banish from
our hearts every desire and thought of evil, that we may truly
revere Thy holy name. Forgive our sins, pardon our failings, and
remove from us suffering and sorrow. May the erring and the
wayward be led to know Thy lovingkindness, and to serve Thee
in newness of heart; and may those who love virtue and do the
right, ever be glad of Thy favor. Bless our land with plenty and
our nation with peace; may righteousness dwell in our midst and
virtue reign among us.

Thou knowest our needs before we utter them, and ordainest
all things for the best. Praised be Thou, O Lord, who hearest
prayer. (*R-1*, p. 349; cf. *O-1*, p. 159)

From Tahanun

. . . Our Father, our King, be gracious unto us and answer us,
for we have no good works of our own; deal with us in charity
for thy Name's sake. Our Lord, our God, hearken to the voice of
our supplications, and remember unto us the covenant of our
fathers, and save us for thy Name's sake. And now, O Lord our
God, thou hast brought thy people forth out of the land of Egypt
with a mighty hand, and hast made thee a name as at this day;

we have sinned, we have done wickedly. O Lord, according to all thy righteous acts, let thine anger and thy fury, I pray thee, be turned away from thy city Jerusalem, thy holy mountain; because for our sins and for the iniquities of our fathers, Jerusalem and thy people are become a byword with all that are around us. Now therefore, hearken, O our God, unto the prayer of thy servant and to his supplications, and cause thy face to shine upon thy sanctuary that is desolate, for the Lord's sake. (*O-1,* p. 171)

O Guardian of Israel, guard the remnant of Israel, and suffer not Israel to perish, who say, Hear, O Israel.

O Guardian for a unique nation, guard the remnant of a unique nation, and suffer not them to perish, who proclaim the unity of Thy Name, saying, The Lord is our God, the Lord is One.

O Guardian of a holy people, guard the remnant of a holy people, and suffer not them to perish, who thrice repeat the threefold sanctification unto the Holy One.

O Thou who art propitiated by prayers for mercy, and art conciliated by supplications, be thou propitious and reconciled to an afflicted generation; for there is none that helpeth. (*O-1,* p. 185)

From Torah service

Blessed art thou, O Lord our God, King of the universe, who hast chosen us from all peoples, and hast given us thy Torah. Blessed art thou, O Lord, Giver of the Torah.

Blessed art thou, O Lord our God, King of the universe, who hast given us the Torah of truth, and hast planted everlasting life in our midst. Blessed art thou, O Lord, Giver of the Torah. (*O-1,* p. 191; cf. *R-1,* pp. 145-46)

Adoration

Let us adore the ever-living God, and render praise unto Him who spread out the heavens and established the earth, whose glory is revealed in the heavens above and whose greatness is manifest throughout the world. He is our God; there is none else.

We bow the head in reverence, and worship the King of kings, the Holy One, praised be He.

May the time not be distant, O God, when Thy name shall be worshiped in all the earth, when unbelief shall disappear and error be no more. Fervently we pray that the day may come when all men shall invoke Thy name, when corruption and evil shall give way to purity and goodness, when superstition shall no longer enslave the mind, nor idolatry blind the eye; when all who dwell on earth shall know that to Thee alone every knee must bend and every tongue give homage. O may all, created in Thine image, recognize that they are brethren, so that, one in spirit and one in fellowship, they may be forever united before Thee. Then shall Thy kingdom be established on earth and the word of Thine ancient seer be fulfilled: The Lord will reign forever and ever.

On that day the Lord shall be One and His name shall be One. (*R-1,* pp. 365-66; cf. *O-1,* p. 209-11)

Kaddish

Magnified and sanctified be his great Name in the world which he hath created according to his will. May he establish his kingdom during your life and during your days, and during the life of all the house of Israel, even speedily and at a near time, and say ye, Amen.

Let his great Name be blessed for ever and to all eternity.

Blessed, praised and glorified, exalted, extolled and honoured, magnified and lauded be the Name of the Holy One, blessed be he; though he be high above all the blessings and hymns, praises and consolations, which are uttered in the world; and say ye, Amen.

Amen.

May there be abundant peace from heaven, and life for us and for all Israel; and say ye, Amen.

Amen.

He who maketh peace in his high places, may he make peace for us and for all Israel; and say ye, Amen. (*O-1,* p. 213; cf. *R-1,* p. 370)

THE EVENING SERVICE (*MA'ARIV*)

(The entire service is found in *O-1*, pp. 302-35; *R-1*, pp. 280-99.)

Bar'hu

Praise ye the Lord, to whom all praise is due.

Praised be the Lord to whom all praise is due forever and ever.

Praised be Thou, O Lord our God, ruler of the world, by whose law the shadows of evening fall and the gates of morn are opened. In wisdom hast Thou established the changes of times and seasons and ordered the ways of the stars in their heavenly courses. Creator of heaven and earth, O living God, rule Thou over us forever. Praised be Thou, O Lord, for the day and its work and for the night and its rest.

Infinite as is Thy power even so is Thy love. Thou didst manifest it through Israel Thy people. By laws and commandments, by statutes and ordinances has Thou led us in the way of righteousness and brought us to the light of truth. Therefore at our lying down and our rising up, we will meditate on Thy teachings and find in Thy laws true life and length of days. O that Thy love may never depart from our hearts. Praised be Thou, O Lord, who hast revealed Thy love through Israel. (*R-1*, p. 288; cf. *O-1*, pp. 305-7)

Hashkivenu

Cause us, O Lord our God, to lie down each night in peace, and to awaken each morning to renewed life and strength. Spread over us the tabernacle of Thy peace. Help us to order our lives by Thy counsel, and lead us in the paths of righteousness. Be Thou a shield about us, protecting us from hate and war, from pestilence and sorrow. Curb Thou also within us the inclination to do evil, and shelter us beneath the shadow of Thy wings. Guard our going out and our coming in unto life and peace from this time forth and for evermore. (*R-1*, p. 56; cf. *O-1*, p. 313)

From the Night Prayer

Blessed be the Lord by day; blessed be the Lord by night; blessed be the Lord when we lie down; blessed be the Lord when we rise up. For in thy hand are the souls of the living and the dead (as it is said), In his hand is the soul of every living thing, and the spirit of all human flesh. Into thy hand I commend my spirit; thou hast redeemed me, O Lord, God of truth. Our God who art in heaven, assert the unity of thy Name, and establish thy kingdom continually, and reign over us for ever and ever. (*O-1,* p. 1003)

From Grace After Meals

Blessed art thou, O Lord our God, King of the universe, who feedest the whole world with thy goodness, with grace, with lovingkindness and tender mercy; thou givest food to all flesh, for thy lovingkindness endureth for ever. Through thy great goodness food hath never failed us: O may it not fail us for ever and ever for thy great Name's sake, since thou nourishest and sustainest all beings, and doest good unto all, and providest food for all thy creatures whom thou hast created. Blessed art thou, O Lord, who givest food unto all. (*O-1,* pp. 967-69)

PART IX

HOLIDAY PRAYERS

"There is no sadness in the presence of God."
—Talmud Hagiga 5b

KEY TO PRAYERBOOKS

Sabbath and holiday services are quoted from the following books:

C-1   *Sabbath and Festival Prayer Book.* The Rabbinical Assembly of America and the United Synagogue of America, The Prayer Book Press, 1946 (Conservative).

C-2   Silverman, Morris, *High Holiday Prayer Book,* (Conservative).

O-1   Hertz, Joseph H., *The Authorized Daily Prayer Book,* Revised Edition, Hebrew Text, English Translation with Commentary and Notes. Bloch Publishing Company, New York, 1948.

O-2   Adler, Naphtali, and Jacob Davis, *Service of the Synagogue,* New Year and Day of Atonement. Hebrew Publishing Company, New York, 1926 (Orthodox).

O-3   Adler, H. M., Israel Zangwill, Arthur Davis, and Nina Salaman, editors, *Festival Services for Passover, Feast of Weeks and Tabernacles.* Hebrew Publishing Company, New York, (no date given—probably 1949) (Orthodox).

O-4   De Sola Pool, David and Tamar, *The Haggadah of Passover.* Jewish Welfare Board, New York, 1943 (Orthodox).

R-1   *The Union Prayerbook for Jewish Worship,* Newly Revised Edition, Part I. The Central Conference of American Rabbis, Cincinnati, 1947, Copyright, 1940 (Reform).

R-2   *The Union Prayerbook for Jewish Worship,* Newly Revised Edition, Part II. New York, the Central Conference of American Rabbis, 1955, Copyright, 1945 (Reform).

R-3   *The Union Haggadah. Home Service for the Passover.* The Central Conference of American Rabbis, Copyright, 1923 (Reform).

Rec-1   *Sabbath Prayer Book.* New York, The Jewish Reconstructionist Foundation, Inc., The Reconstructionist Press, 1953.

Rec-2   *High Holiday Prayer Book,* Volume I: *Prayers for Rosh Hashanah.* New York, The Jewish Reconstructionist Foundation, Inc., The Reconstructionist Press, 1948.

Rec-3   *High Holiday Prayer Book,* Volume II: *Prayers for Yom Kippur.* New York, The Jewish Reconstructionist Foundation, Inc., The Reconstructionist Press, 1948.

Rec-4   Kaplan, Mordecai M., Eugene Kohn, and Ira Eisenstein, *The New Haggadah.* New York, Behrman House, Inc., 1942.

Prayers are quoted from the various editions of the Prayerbook. Inconsistencies in spelling, translation, or transliteration are due to the different methods used by authors and publishers.

THE SABBATH SERVICE

Beloved, come, the bride to meet,
The Princess Sabbath let us greet.

Come, to the Sabbath greetings bring,
For it is blessings constant spring:
Of old ordained, divinely taught,
Last in creation, first in thought.

Arouse thyself, awake and shine,
Thy light has come, the light divine;
Awake and sing, and over thee
The glory of the Lord shall be.

Crown of thy husband, come in peace;
Let joy and gladsome song increase.
Among His faithful, sorrow-tried,
His chosen people, come, O bride.

Beloved, come, the bride to meet,
The Princess Sabbath let us greet.
("*L'cha Dodi,*" *R-1,* pp. 26-27;
cf. *O-1,* pp. 356-359)

Our God, and God of our Fathers, grant that our worship on this Sabbath be acceptable to Thee. Sanctify us through Thy commandments, and may we share in the blessings of Thy word. Teach us to be satisfied with the gifts of Thy goodness and gratefully to rejoice in all Thy mercies. Purify our hearts that we may serve Thee in truth. O help us to preserve the Sabbath as Israel's heritage from generation to generation, that it may bring rest and joy, peace and comfort to the dwellings of our brethren, and through it Thy name be hallowed in all the earth. Praised be Thou, O Lord, who sanctifiest the Sabbath!

(*R-1,* p. 22; cf. *O-1,* pp. 380-83)

Sanctification of the Sabbath—Kiddush

Praised art Thou, O Lord our God, King of the universe who createst the fruit of the vine.

Praised art Thou, O Lord our God, Ruler of the universe, who hast sanctified us through Thy commandments and hast taken delight in us. In love and favor Thou hast given us the holy Sabbath as a heritage, a reminder of Thy work of creation, first of our sacred days recalling our liberation from Egypt. Thou didst choose us from among the peoples and in Thy love and favor didst sanctify us in giving us Thy holy Sabbath as a joyous heritage. Blessed art Thou, O Lord our God, who hallowest the Sabbath.

(*C-1,* p. 28; cf. *O-1,* p. 409; *R-1,* p. 93)

Every living soul shall praise Thee; the spirit of all flesh shall glorify Thy name. Thou art God from everlasting to everlasting and besides Thee there is no redeemer nor savior. Thou art the first and the last, the Lord of all generations. Thou rulest the world in kindness and all Thy creatures in mercy. Thou art our guardian who sleepest not and slumberest not. To Thee alone we give thanks. Yet though our lips overflow with song, and our tongues with joyous praise, we should still be unable to thank Thee even for a thousandth part of the bounties which Thou hast bestowed upon our fathers and upon us. Thou hast been our protector and our savior in every trial and peril. Thy mercy has watched over us, and Thy lovingkindness has never failed us.

(*R-1,* p. 105; cf. *C-1,* pp. 84-85; *O-1,* pp. 416-19)

Thou didst establish the Sabbath and didst accept its offerings, prescribing the order of its service. They that delight in the Sabbath have a glorious heritage; they who partake of it merit life's

highest joy and they that love its observance have thus chosen
true distinction. . . . May they who observe the Sabbath and call
it a delight rejoice in Thy kingdom. May the people who sanctify
the seventh day be sated and delighted with Thy bounty. For
Thou didst find pleasure in the seventh day, and didst sanctify
it, calling it the most desirable of days, in remembrance of
creation.

(*C-1*, pp. 140-142; cf. *O-1*, pp. 530-33)

> Thou art One, Thy name is one
> And who is like Thy people Israel,
> Unique on earth?
>
> A crown of distinction, a crown of salvation
> The Sabbath Thou gavest us
>
> For the spirit's re-birth.
> Our fathers have told us that on the Sabbath day,
> Abraham and Isaac rejoiced: Jacob and his sons
> Found joy and rest.
>
> This day of true peace, this day of delight,
> Granted in love for tranquil repose,
> By Thee was blest.
>
> May Thy children know that from Thee cometh rest.
> In observing the Sabbath, choicest of days,
> They hallow Thy name.
> (From the Sabbath Afternoon Service, *C-1*, p. 171;
> cf. *O-1*, pp. 578-79; paraphrase in *R-1*, p. 162)

The Havdalah Service

The father raises the cup of wine and says:

Behold, God is my salvation; I will trust, and will not be afraid,
for the Lord is my strength and song and He is become my salvation. Ye shall draw waters with joy from the wells of salvation.
Salvation belongs to the Lord; Thy blessing be upon Thy people. The Lord of hosts is with us; the God of Jacob is our refuge.

. . . I will lift the cup of salvation and call upon the name of the Lord.

Blessed art Thou, O Lord our God, King of the universe, who createst the fruit of the vine!

He raises the spice box and says:

Blessed art Thou, O Lord our God, King of the universe, who createst divers kinds of spices.

He spreads his hands toward the Havdalah candle and says:

Blessed art Thou, O Lord our God, King of the universe, who createst the light of the fire!

He again raises the cup and says:

Blessed art Thou, O Lord our God, King of the universe, who makest a distinction between the holy and the profane, between light and darkness, between Israel and the nations, between the seventh day and the six working days. Blessed art Thou, O Lord, who makest a distinction between the holy and the profane.

(*O-1,* pp. 744-49; *C-1,* p. 262)

In Remembrance of the Ancient Temple Service

In ancient days, the Temple in Jerusalem was the symbol of God's presence. There sacrifices were offered daily in behalf of the entire nation. On the Sabbath a special sacrifice marked the day's holiness. Thus did the Temple bear testimony to Israel's consecration to the God of all mankind.

The Temple has long since been destroyed, yet the remembrance of it lives on in the heart of our people. The form of worship practiced there belongs to a bygone age, yet it continues to awaken solemn thoughts.

Today Israel is scattered in many lands. But when we remember the Temple, we feel that we are part of one people, dedicated to the service of God and His kingdom of righteousness.

Our worship is one of prayer and praise. But when we think of the piety of our fathers who from their meager store of cattle and grain, the yield of the shepherd's care and the farmer's toil, offered their best in the service of God, can we be content with a gift of mere words that costs us neither labor nor privation? Shall we not feel impelled to devote of our substance to the service of God? Shall we not give of our store to the relief of suffering, the healing of sickness, the dispelling of ignorance and error, the righting of wrongs and the strengthening of faith?

(Rec-1, pp. 189-191)

A Sabbath Prayer

Almighty and merciful God, Thou hast called Israel to Thy service and found him worthy to bear witness unto Thy truth among the peoples of the earth. Give us grace to fulfil this mission with zeal tempered by wisdom and guided by regard for other men's faith. May our life prove the strength of our own belief in the truths we proclaim. May our bearing toward our neighbors, our faithfulness in every sphere of duty, our compassion for the suffering and our patience under trial show that He whose law we obey is indeed the God of all goodness, the Father of all men, that to serve Him is perfect freedom and to worship Him the soul's purest happiness.

O Lord, open our eyes that we may see and welcome all truth, whether shining from the annals of ancient revelations or reaching us through the seers of our own time; for Thou hidest not Thy light from any generation of Thy children that yearn for Thee and seek Thy guidance.

We pray for the masters and teachers in Israel that they may dispense Thy truth with earnestness and zeal, yet not without charity. May the law of love be found on their lips, and may they by precept and example lead many in the ways of righteousness.

Bless, O God, all endeavors, wherever made, to lift up the fallen, to redeem the sinful, to bring back those who wander from the right path and restore them to a worthy life.

Endow us with purity of heart and steadfastness of spirit that our lives may testify of Thee and sanctify Thy name. O satisfy us early with Thy mercy, that we may rejoice and be glad all our days. Amen.

(R-1, pp. 34-35)

Prayer for the Government of the United States

Fervently we invoke Thy blessing upon our country and our nation. Guard them, O God, from calamity and injury; suffer not their adversaries to triumph over them, but let the glories of a just, righteous and God-fearing people increase from age to age. Enlighten with Thy wisdom and sustain with Thy power those whom the people have set in authority, the President, his counselors, and advisers, the judges, law-givers and executives, and all who are entrusted with our safety and with the guardianship of our rights and our liberties. May peace and good-will obtain among all the inhabitants of our land; may religion spread its blessings among us and exalt our nation in righteousness. Amen.

(*R-1*, p. 148; cf. *C-1*, p. 130; *O-1*, p. 507)

The *Orthodox* Sabbath Eve Service may be found in *O-1*, pp. 342-413; the Sabbath Morning Service on pp. 416-563; the Sabbath Afternoon Service on pp. 570-723, including extensive readings from the Psalms and from the Mishna, Tractate, Ethics of the Fathers, for Sabbath afternoon study; the evening service for the Conclusion of Sabbath, pp. 724-53.

The *Conservative* Sabbath Eve Service opens *C-1* on pp. 5-41, followed by the Sabbath Morning Service, pp. 42-162; the Afternoon Service, pp. 163-76; and the evening service for the Conclusion of the Sabbath, pp. 238-62.

The *Reform* worship service is presented in the *R-1*, with five Sabbath Eve services for the four or five Friday evenings of the month, on pp. 8-99; the Morning Service, pp. 100-55; the Afternoon Service, pp. 157-78.

SERVICE FOR THE NEW MOON

Announcement of the New Moon

Almighty God, grant that the approaching month of —— which begins —— of the coming week, may be a messenger of

good tidings to us all. Bestow upon us a life of health and peace,
of sustenance and contentment. Help us to spend this month in
the love of Thee and in the service of man, and so to order our
way that it may be pleasing in Thy sight. Amen.

(*R-1*, p. 147)

Meditation

O heavenly Father, the approach of another month reminds
us of the flight of time and the change of seasons. Month follows
month; the years of man's life are few and fleeting. Teach us to
number our days that we may use each precious moment wisely.
May no day pass without bringing us closer to some worthy
achievement. Grant that the new month bring life and hope, joy
and peace to all Thy children. Amen.

(*C-1*, p. 129)

From the Additional Service for the New Moon

New moons didst Thou assign unto Thy people as seasons of
atonement throughout their generations. May they be a memorial
of the sacrifices and sin offerings formerly offered unto Thee for
atonement and for the salvation of their souls from the hand of
the enemy. O, establish a new altar on Zion, and we will offer
upon it the burnt offering of the New Moon. We will rejoice in
the service of the sanctuary, and in the songs of David thy servant
which shall then be heard in Thy city and chanted before Thine
altar. . . .

Our God and God of our fathers, renew this month unto us
for good and for blessing, for joy and gladness, for salvation and
consolation, for support and sustenance, for life and peace, for
pardon of sin and forgiveness of iniquity; for Thou hast chosen
Thy people Israel from all nations, and hast appointed unto
them statutes for the New Moons. Blessed art Thou, O Lord,
who sanctifiest Israel and the New Moons.

(*O-1*, pp. 779-83)

The *Orthodox* Service for the New Moon provides for inclusion of special prayers in the daily morning service and
the addition of an entire section known as *musaf* or addi-

tional service, when the New Moon occurs on a weekday (*O-1*, pp. 148, 776-87). The Torah is taken from the Ark, and a portion from Numbers 28: 1-15 is read. Similarly, when the New Moon occurs on the Sabbath, special prayers are included in the service, the additional service for the Sabbath is altered, and a second Torah scroll is taken from the Ark for the reading of the passage from Numbers (*O-1*, pp. 460-63, 542-45).

Conservative synagogues which conduct daily services follow Orthodox practice for New Moon on weekdays. For New Moons occurring on the Sabbath prayers vary slightly from the Orthodox pattern (*C-1*, pp. 99, 110-15, 140-42).

SERVICE FOR THE NEW YEAR

Our God and God of our fathers, reign over all the universe in Thy glory, and in Thy splendor be exalted over all the earth. Shine forth in the majesty of Thy triumphant power over all the inhabitants of Thy world, that every living creature may understand that Thou hast created it, and all with life's breath in their nostrils may declare: "The Lord, God of Israel, is King and His dominion rules over all." Our God and God of our fathers, sanctify us by Thy commandments and grant that our portion be in Thy Torah; satisfy us with Thy goodness and gladden us with Thy salvation. Purify our hearts that we may serve Thee in truth, for Thou, O God, art Truth, and Thy word is truth and endures forever. Blessed art Thou, O Lord, Thou King over all the earth, who sanctifiest Israel and the Day of Remembrance.

(From the morning service, *C-2*, p. 75; cf. *R-2*, p. 58; *O-2*, p. 93)

And thus, all shall acclaim sovereignty unto God:
Unto God who orders judgment,
Who searches hearts on the Day of Judgment
Who uncovers deep things in judgment,
Who ordains righteousness on the Day of Judgment;
Who utters knowledge in judgment,

Who is perfect and shows mercy on the Day of Judgment;
Who remembers His covenant in judgment,
Who has compassion upon His handiwork in the Day of
    Judgment;
Who purifies those who trust in Him in judgment,
Who divines men's thoughts on the Day of Judgment;
Who restrains His indignation on the Day of Judgment,
Who is clothed in charity on the Day of Judgment;
Who pardons iniquities in judgment,
Who is revered in praises on the Day of Judgment.

> (From the morning service, *C-2*, p. 89;
> cf. *O-2*, p. 106)

Our Father, our King, hear our prayer.
Our Father, our King, we have sinned before Thee.
Our Father, our King, keep far from our country pestilence, war
    and famine.
Our Father, our King, cause all hate and oppression to vanish
    from the earth.
Our Father, our King, inscribe us for blessing in the book of life.
Our Father, our King, grant unto us a year of happiness.

> (From the morning service, *R-2*, p. 62; cf. *C-2*,
> pp. 94-96; *O-2*, pp. 11-13)

The *Orthodox* service for the New Year includes a relatively brief service at sundown on the eve of the festival, with a pattern similar to the Sabbath eve service except for a few special prayers for the New Year. The service on the eve of the second day is identical with the first. The afternoon services on both the first and second days likewise are brief. The morning services on both days, however, are elaborate. The central prayer of the additional service—which consists of seven benedictions on the Sabbath and all other holidays —is expanded to nine benedictions. The cantor, frequently assisted by an a capella choir, chants the many medieval hymns, written in flowery Hebrew, known as *Piyutim*, which further embellish the New Year service. Special prayers also introduce the blowing of the *shofar* immediately after the Torah service and during the additional service. The entire first section of *O-2* with its 526 pages—263 Hebrew and 263 English translation—is devoted to the New Year services.

Conservative services follow a similar pattern, except that many of the medieval hymns whose Hebrew poetry is quite strange to the twentieth-century mind are omitted. Some of the prayers are recited in English. Some Conservative synagogues have organs and mixed choirs. Most of these synagogues use *C-2*, where the New Year service fills 382 pages, half of which are in Hebrew and half in English.

The *Reform* Jewish service is brief by contrast. The holiday is observed for one day only and *R-2* provides for services for the eve and the morning of the festival. The 93 pages of material include some of the traditional prayers in Hebrew, others in English paraphrase. Many of the Orthodox prayers are omitted altogether, while new prayers, expressing the ideas of the festival in the language of our time, are added in English.

PENITENTIAL PRAYERS

The Orthodox synagogue has a special book of penitential prayers known as *S'lihot*. Special prayers for the days preceding and following the New Year were composed mostly during the Middle Ages. Each prayer culminates in the following refrain which is also used in the liturgy for the Day of Atonement:

Almighty King, enthroned in mercy and governing Thy people with loving-kindness, Thou causest their sins to pass away one by one. Thou art ever ready to extend Thy pardon to sinners, and forgiveness to transgressors, judging charitably all the living, and not requiting them according to the evil they do. O God, who has taught us to repeat Thy thirteen attributes, remember unto

us this day the covenant of Thy mercy in these attributes, as
Thou didst reveal them of old to Moses, the humble, in the
words written in the Torah: "And the Lord descended in the
cloud and stood with him there, and proclaimed the name of
the Lord."

And the Lord passed before him and proclaimed: The Lord,
the Lord is a compassionate and gracious God, slow to anger,
abundant in loving-kindness and truth; keeping mercy for thousands, forgiving iniquity, transgression and sin, and acquitting
the penitent.

O Pardon our iniquity and our sin, and take us for Thy heritage. Forgive us, O our Father, for we have sinned; pardon us,
our King, for we have transgressed. For Thou, O Lord, art good,
and ready to forgive, and art abundant in mercy unto all them
that call upon Thee.

(C-2, p. 380; cf. O-2, p. 177)

On this Sabbath of Repentance, O our God, open our hearts
to its solemn call to turn from the vanities of life and consider
our destiny in the light of Thine eternal truth. Help us to see
whether we have indeed hearkened to Thy voice within us, and
have done justly, loved mercy and walked humbly before Thee,
or whether we have been negligent in the fulfilment of our duties
and have strayed from the path of rectitude.

Humbly we confess that our intentions and our deeds accuse
us before the tribunal of our conscience and convict us in Thy
sight, O righteous Judge of the world. Help us to remove every
misunderstanding between ourselves and our fellowmen. O God,
who art plenteous in mercy and forgiveness, do Thou establish
peace and harmony within our souls, that we may be truly at one
with Thee. Amen.

(From the prayer for the Sabbath of Repentance
R-1, p. 137)

FROM THE ATONEMENT DAY SERVICE

Our God and God of our fathers, pardon our transgressions,
remove our guilt and blot out our iniquities on this Day of

Atonement, as Thou hast promised: I, even I, blot out thine iniquities for Mine own sake, and thy sins will I remember no more. I have made thy sins to vanish like a cloud and thy transgressions like a mist; return to Me for I have redeemed thee. For on this day shall ye be forgiven and cleansed from all your sins; before the Lord shall ye be clean.

(R-2, p. 222; cf. C-2, p. 268; O-2, p. 24)

For the sin which we have sinned against Thee under stress or through choice;

For the sin which we have sinned against Thee openly or in secret;

For the sin which we have sinned against Thee in stubbornness or in error;

For the sin which we have sinned against Thee in the evil meditation of the heart;

For the sin which we have sinned against Thee by the word of mouth;

For the sin which we have sinned against Thee by abuse of power;

For the sin which we have sinned against Thee by the profanation of Thy name;

For the sin which we have sinned against Thee by disrespect for parents and teachers;

For the sin which we have sinned against Thee by exploiting or dealing treacherously with our neighbor.

For all these sins, O God of forgiveness, bear with us, pardon us, forgive us.

(R-2, pp. 224-26; cf. C-2, pp. 270-72; O-2, pp. 26-28)

Thou hast distinguished man from the beginning and hast singled him out to stand before Thee. Yet who dare say unto Thee, what doest Thou? And though man be righteous, what does he give to Thee? In Thy love Thou hast given us this Day of Atonement for the remission and pardon of all our sins, that we may refrain from every form of exploitation and return to Thee to do Thy will with a perfect heart. Have pity upon us in Thy great mercy for it is not Thy desire that mankind should be destroyed. As it is said, Seek ye the Lord while He may be found, call ye upon Him while He is near; let the wicked forsake his ways, and the unrighteous man his evil thoughts, and let him return unto the Lord, who will have mercy upon him and to our God, who will abundantly pardon. Yea, Thou art merciful and gracious, long-suffering and of infinite patience and faithfulness; Thou acceptest with favor the repentance of the wicked and desirest not their death, as Thy prophet has spoken: Say to them, As I live, saith the Lord God, I have no pleasure in the death of the wicked, but that the wicked turn from his way and live; turn ye, turn ye from your evil ways; for why will ye die, O house of Israel? Have I any pleasure at all that the wicked should die? saith the Lord God; and not rather that he should return from his ways and live?

(R-2, pp. 340-42; cf. C-2, p. 456; O-2, p. 251)

The same difference between Orthodox, Conservative, and Reform services described in connection with the New Year service apply on the Day of Atonement. The Orthodox service in the Atonement section of *O-2* covers 736 pages; the Conservative service in *C-2*, 618 pages; the Reform service in *R-2*, 256 pages.

FROM THE PRAYERS FOR THE FESTIVAL OF BOOTHS

Blessed art Thou, O Lord our God, King of the universe, who hast chosen us for Thy service from among all peoples. Thou hast exalted us and sanctified us by Thy commandments. In love Thou hast given us holidays for gladness, festivals for rejoicing. Thou hast granted us this Feast of Booths, the Season of our Gladness, as a holy convocation, commemorating our liberation from Egypt. Thou hast chosen us and sanctified us from among all peoples. Thou hast given us Thy holy festivals as a joyous heritage. Blessed art Thou, O Lord, who hallowest Israel and the Festivals.

(From the Kiddush, C-1, p. 35; O-1, pp. 808-11;
R-1, pp. 206-08)

> For Thy sake, our God, do Thou save us.
> For Thy sake, our Creator, O save us.
> For Thy sake, our Redeemer, O save us.
> For Thy sake, O Thou who seekest us, save us.

Save Thy people, and bless Thine inheritance; nourish and sustain them forever. And may my words of supplication before the Lord be nigh unto the Lord our God, day and night, that He maintain the cause of His servant and the cause of His people Israel, as every day shall require; that all the people of the earth may know that the Lord is God; there is none else.

> (From the processional prayers of
> supplication *C-1,* p. 191)

Thou, O Lord, art the source of life, the fountain of light and of truth. Let Thy doctrine descend as the rain, Thy word distil as the dew. Open Thou our hearts that they may receive the good seeds of Thine instruction, and let Thy blessing ripen them into fruits of righteousness. Let Thy gracious promise be fulfilled: I will pour water upon the thirsty land and streams upon the dry ground; I will pour My spirit upon thy seed and My blessing upon thine offspring.

> Let rain and dew descend upon the fields of our land,
> For the blessing of all and the hurt of none;
> For the joy of all and the woe of none;
> For the life of all and the death of none.

> (From the Prayer for Rain, Feast
> of Conclusion, *R-1,* p. 265)

The order of service for *Succot,* as well as for the festivals of Passover and Pentecost, is very similar to that of the Sabbath. In each service the central prayer, the *Amidah,* assumes the form typical of these three festivals, with the name of the festival inserted in the fourth of the seven blessings. The Orthodox Prayerbook provides medieval *Piyutim* for inclusion in each of the services. These are retained only in part in the Conservative service while, in the Reform Prayerbook, they are replaced by contemporary prayers reflecting the meaning of the festival.

Characteristics of the *Succot* liturgy are the petitions recited during the daily processions during the intermediate days of the festival and, particularly, during the seventh day, *Hashana Rabbah.* Prayers for rain are recited on the eighth day, *Sh'mini Atzeret.* They are included in the *Musaf* or additional section of the morning service in the Orthodox and Conservative synagogues while, in the Reform synagogue, they are recited immediately after the Torah reading.

An outline of the Orthodox *Succot* service may be found in *O-1,* pp. 788-828. The services for *Succot,* in every detail, are contained in *O-3.*

C-1 includes the festival liturgy with the Sabbath services. Special prayers for the Three Festivals are on pp. 29, 102, 110, 146, 178.

For use in Reform synagogues, *R-1* offers evening and morning services for the festivals as a separate section on pp. 181-277.

FROM THE PROCESSIONAL HYMNS FOR *SIMHAT TORAH*

We beseech Thee, O Lord, save us.

We beseech Thee, O Lord, do Thou cause us to prosper.

O Lord, answer us in the day that we call.

God of all souls save us.
Thou who searchest hearts, do Thou cause us to prosper.
Thou mighty Redeemer, answer us in the day that we call.

Thou who knowest our thoughts, save us.
Mighty and resplendent God, do Thou cause us to prosper.
Thou who art clothed in righteousness, answer us in the day that
we call.

Thou who helpest the poor, save us.
O Redeemer and Deliverer, do Thou cause us to prosper.
Thou Rock of Ages, answer us in the day that we call.

. . .   .

I will rejoice and exult on *Simhat Torah.* The Branch of David
(Messiah) will surely come on *Simhat Torah.*

The Torah is a tree of life; it is life to all; for with Thee is the
fountain of life.

Abraham, Isaac and Jacob rejoiced on *Simhat Torah.*

Moses rejoiced on *Simhat Torah.*

Aaron, Joshua, Samuel, David and Solomon rejoiced on *Simhat
Torah.*

The Torah is a tree of life: it is life to all; for with
Thee is the fountain of life.

(C-1, pp. 216-19; cf. *R-1,* pp.
260-64; *O-3,* p. 108)

With exception of the special prayers for the Torah service
and its elaborate processional, the prayers for *Simhat Torah*
are like those for the eighth day of *Succot.*

Since the festival is postbiblical in origin, there is no mention of it in the Scriptures.

FROM THE CANDLE-LIGHTING SERVICE FOR *HANUKKAH*

We kindle these lights on account of the miracles, the deliverances and the wonders which Thou didst work for our fathers by
means of Thy holy priests. During all the eight days of Hanukah
these lights are sacred, neither is it permitted us to make any
profane use of them; but we are only to look at them, in order
that we may give thanks unto Thy Name for Thy miracles, Thy
deliverances and Thy wonders.

(O-1, p. 948; *C-1,* p. 264)

Rock of Ages, let our song praise Thy saving power;
Thou amidst the raging foes, wast our shelt'ring tower.

Furious they assailed us, but Thine arm availed us,
And Thy word broke their sword
When our own strength failed us.

Children of the martyr-race, whether free or fettered,
Wake the echoes of the songs, where ye may be scattered.
Yours the message cheering that the time is nearing
Which will see all men free,
Tyrants disappearing.

(C-1, p. 365; *R-1,* p. 92)

Hanukkah Prayer Added to the Daily Service

We thank Thee also for the miracles, for the redemption, for
the mighty deeds and saving acts, wrought by Thee, as well as for
the wars which Thou didst wage for our fathers in days of old,
at this season.

In the days of the Hasmonean, Mattathias, son of Johanan,
the High Priest and his sons, when the iniquitous power of
Greece rose up against Thy people Israel to make them forgetful
of Thy Torah, and to force them to transgress the statutes of
Thy will, then didst Thou in Thine abundant mercy rise up for
them in the time of their trouble; Thou didst plead their cause,
Thou didst judge their suit, Thou didst avenge their wrong;
Thou deliveredst the strong into the hands of the weak, the many
into the hands of the few, the impure into the hands of the pure,
the wicked into the hands of the righteous, and the arrogant into
the hands of them that occupied themselves with Thy Torah:
for thyself Thou didst make a great and holy name in Thy
world, and for Thy people Israel Thou didst work a great deliverance and redemption as at this day. And thereupon Thy children came into the inner sanctuary of Thy house, cleansed Thy
temple, purified Thy holy place, kindled lights in Thy sacred
courts, and appointed these eight days of Hanukah in order to
give thanks and praises unto Thy great Name.

(O-1, pp. 150-53; *C-1,* p. 100)

The service for *Hanukkah* may be found in *O-1,* pp. 946-
52; in *C-1,* pp. 263, 365; and in *R-1,* pp. 85-92.

The story of *Hanukkah*, in its original form, may be found
in the First and Second Books of Maccabees in any edition of
the Apocrypha.

THE BOOK OF ESTHER

Fast Into Feast

Now in the days of Ahasuerus—this is the Ahasuerus who
reigned from India to Ethiopia, over a hundred and twenty-seven
provinces—the king, in the third year of his reign, gave a feast for
all the princes and nobles of his provinces, and showed them the
riches of his glorious kingdom for a hundred and fourscore days.

When these days had passed, the king gave for all the people
who were present in Shushan a seven-day feast in the court of
the garden of the king's palace. There were hangings of white
cotton and blue, fastened with cords of fine linen and purple
upon silver rings and pillars of marble; and the couches were of
gold and silver, upon a pavement of green and white and shell
and onyx. The drinks were served in vessels of gold, each vessel
different one from another, and royal wine in abundance.

Vashti the queen also gave a feast for the women in the royal
house which belonged to King Ahasuerus.

On the seventh day, when the heart of the king was merry with
wine, he ordered his seven chamberlains to bring Vashti the
queen before the king wearing the crown royal, to show the people and the princes her beauty, for she was fair to look upon.
But the queen Vashti refused to come at the king's command by
his chamberlains. Therefore the king became enraged, and his
anger burned within him.

The king asked the wise men, who knew the times, "What
shall we do to the queen Vashti, according to law, because she
has not obeyed the command of the king?"

And one answered, "Vashti the queen has done wrong not
only to the king, but also to all the princes and people in the
provinces of the king Ahasuerus. For when this deed of the queen
becomes known to all women, it will cause them to disobey their
husbands. If it please the king, let a royal decree be sent out, and

written among the laws of the Persians and the Medes, so that it may not be altered, that Vashti come no more before King Ahasuerus, and that the king give her royal estate to another better than she. Thus when the king's decree is proclaimed throughout his empire, all wives will give honor to their husbands, both to high and low."

This saying pleased the king and the princes. And the king sent letters to every province, to every people in their own language, so that every man should rule in his own house.

After these things, when the wrath of King Ahasuerus subsided, he remembered Vashti and what she had done, and what was decreed against her.

Then said the king's servants who ministered to him, "Let fair young maidens be sought for the king. And let the king appoint officers in all the provinces of his kingdom to gather together all the fair young maidens at the palace, in the custody of Hegai, the king's chamberlain, keeper of the women. And let the maiden who pleases the king best be queen instead of Vashti."

Now in Shushan there was a certain Jew named Mordecai, a Benjamite who had been carried away from Jerusalem with the captives taken by Nebuchadnezzar. And Mordecai brought up Hadassah, called Esther, his uncle's daughter, for she had neither father nor mother. And the maiden was fair to look upon.

So it came to pass, when the king's decree was proclaimed, and when many maidens assembled in Shushan, that Esther also was brought to the king's house, to the custody of Hegai.

The maiden pleased Hegai, and she obtained kindness from him; and he speedily gave her seven maidens from the king's house to serve her; and he assigned her and her maidens to the best place in the house of women.

Now when each maiden's turn came to go to the king Ahasuerus, whatever she desired was given her when she left the house of the women. In the evening she went; and on the morrow she returned to the second house of the women, where dwelt the concubines. She came no more to the king, unless the king delighted in her and she was called by name.

When the turn came for Esther to go to the king, she asked for nothing but what Hegai appointed. And Esther obtained favor in the sight of all those who looked upon her. So Esther went to King Ahasuerus in his house royal, in the seventh year of his reign. And the king loved Esther above all the women, and she obtained grace and favor in his sight more than all the others, so that he set the royal crown upon her head and made her queen instead of Vashti.

Then the king gave a great feast for all his princes and servants, a feast for Esther; and he proclaimed a holiday and distributed gifts.

And when the maidens were gathered together the second time, then Mordecai sat at the king's gate. Esther had not yet made known to the king her kindred or her people, as Mordecai had charged her; for Esther did the bidding of Mordecai just as when she was brought up by him.

In those days, while Mordecai sat at the king's gate, two of the king's chamberlains, Bigthan and Teresh, who guarded the door, sought to lay hands on the king. The matter became known to Mordecai, who told it to Esther the queen; and Esther informed the king in Mordecai's name. And when the matter was examined it was found to be so. Therefore Bigthan and Teresh were both hanged on a tree; and it was recorded in the Book of Chronicles in the presence of the king.

After these events King Ahasuerus promoted Haman, the son of Hammedatha the Agagite, and set him above all the princes. And the king's servants who were at the king's gate bowed down before Haman, for the king had so commanded concerning him. But Mordecai bowed not, nor did him honor.

Then the king's servants asked Mordecai, "Why do you ignore the king's command?" They spoke daily to him, and when he paid no heed to them, they told Haman. When Haman saw that Mordecai bowed not, he was full of wrath. But he scorned the thought of laying hands on Mordecai alone, for they had told him of Mordecai's people. Wherefore Haman sought to destroy all the Jews, the people of Mordecai, throughout the kingdom of Ahasuerus.

Then Haman said to the king, "There is a certain people scattered abroad and dispersed in all the provinces of your kingdom; and their laws are different from other peoples': neither do they keep the king's laws. Therefore it is not to the king's profit to suffer them to live. If it please the king, let it be decreed that they may be destroyed; and I will pay ten thousand talents of silver to those in charge of this matter, to bring into the king's treasury."

The king took his ring from his hand, and gave it to Haman, the enemy of the Jews, and said, "The silver is yours, and the people also, to do with them as seems good to you."

Then the king's scribes were called, and a decree was issued according to that which Haman had ordered; and it was sent to the governor in each province, according to the writing and language of the people. And it was written in the name of the king, and sealed with the king's ring.

And the letters were sent by posts into all the king's provinces, to destroy, to kill, and to cause to perish all Jews, both young and old, little children and women, in one day, upon the thirteenth day of the twelfth month, which is the month of Adar, the day set by the *pur*, which is the lot cast. The posts went out, being hastened by the king's command, and the decree was given in Shushan the palace.

And the king and Haman sat down to drink; but the city Shushan was perplexed.

When Mordecai learned of all that was done, he rent his clothes and put on sackcloth and ashes. He went into the midst of the city and cried out loud and bitterly; and came even before the king's gate, though none might enter the king's gate when clothed in sackcloth. And in every province, wherever the king's decree came, there was great mourning among the Jews, and fasting and weeping and wailing, and many lay in sackcloth and ashes.

When Esther's maids came and told her, the queen was grieved. She sent garments to clothe Mordecai, and to take away his sackcloth; but he accepted them not. Then Esther summoned Hatach, one of the king's chamberlains, whom he had appointed to attend her, and sent him secretly to Mordecai to find out why he was in mourning. Hatach went to Mordecai before the king's gate; and Mordecai told him of all that had happened, and of the sum of money that Haman had promised to pay to the king's treasury for the destruction of the Jews. Also he gave him the copy of the decree that was issued from Shushan to show to Esther, and to charge her to go to the king and plead for her people.

Hatach returned and told Esther the words of Mordecai. Again Esther sent word with Hatach to Mordecai: "All the king's people know the law that whoever, whether man or woman, comes to the king into the inner court without being summoned, he is put to death, except those to whom the king holds out the golden scepter, that he may live. But I have not been called to the king these thirty days."

Then Mordecai sent this answer to Esther: "Think not that you shall escape in the king's house, any more than all the Jews. For if you hold your peace at this time, then deliverance shall arise to the Jews from another source, but you and your father's house shall be destroyed. For who knows whether you have not come to the kingdom for just such a time as this?"

Esther bade them return to Mordecai this reply: "Go, gather together all the Jews who are in Shushan, and fast for me three days, and I and my maidens will fast also. Then will I go to the king unbidden. And if I perish, I perish."

So Mordecai went his way, and did all that Esther had commanded him.

On the third day Esther put on her royal apparel, and stood in the inner court of the king's house. And when the king, who sat upon his royal throne, saw Esther the queen standing in the court, she obtained favor in his sight, and the king held out to Esther the golden scepter in his hand.

Then the king asked, "What is your request, Queen Esther? It shall be given you, even to the half of my kingdom." And Esther answered, "If it seem good to the king, let the king and Haman come tomorrow to the banquet that I have prepared for them."

Then Haman went out that day joyful and with a glad heart.

But when he saw Mordecai at the king's gate, and that he neither stood up nor moved for him, he was full of indignation. Nevertheless, Haman restrained himself. And when he came home, he sent for his friends, and Zeresh his wife. And Haman told them of the glory of his riches, and all the things in which the king had advanced him above the princes.

Moreover, Haman said, "Esther the queen lets no man come with the king to the banquets she prepares, but tomorrow I am invited also with the king. Yet all this avails me nothing, so long as I see Mordecai the Jew sitting at the king's gate."

Then said Zeresh his wife and all his friends, "Let a gallows be made fifty cubits high, and tomorrow speak to the king that Mordecai may be hanged on it. Then go in merrily with the king to the banquet."

The counsel pleased Haman, and he caused the gallows to be made.

On the night before the banquet the king could not sleep. And he asked for the Book of the Chronicles, and they read it to him. And in it was found written that Mordecai had told of Bigthan and Teresh, the king's chamberlains who had sought to lay hands on the king Ahasuerus.

The king asked, "What honor has been done to Mordecai for this?" Then answered the king's servants, "Nothing has been done for him." And the king asked, "Who is in the court?" Now Haman had come into the outer court of the king's house, to speak to the king to hang Mordecai on the gallows which had been prepared. And the king's servants answered, "Behold, Haman stands in the court." The king said, "Let him come in." So Haman came in.

And the king said to Haman, "What shall be done for the man whom the king wishes to honor?" Now Haman thought to himself, "Whom would the king wish to honor other than myself?" And Haman answered the king, "For the man whom the king wishes to honor, let the royal apparel be brought which the king wears, and the horse which the king rides upon, and the crown royal which is set upon his head; and let the horse and apparel be delivered to the hand of one of the king's most noble princes, that he may array the man whom the king wishes to honor, and bring him on horseback through the streets of the city and proclaim before him: 'Thus is it done to the man whom the king wishes to honor.' "

Then the king answered, "Make haste, and take the apparel and the horse, as you have said, and do so to Mordecai the Jew, who sits at the king's gate. Let nothing fail of all that you have spoken!"

Haman took the apparel and the horse, and arrayed Mordecai, and brought him on horseback through the streets of the city, and proclaimed before him, "Thus is it done to the man whom the king wishes to honor!"

Then Mordecai returned to the king's gate. But Haman hastened to his home like one in mourning, with his head covered; and he told Zeresh his wife and his friends everything that had befallen him. And while they were still talking with him, the king's chamberlains came to bring Haman to the banquet which Esther had prepared.

So the king and Haman came to banquet with Esther the queen.

And the king said again to Esther at the banquet of wine, "What is your request, Queen Esther? It shall be granted to you, even to the half of my kingdom."

Then Esther the queen answered, "If I have found favor in your eyes, O King, let my life be spared me at my petition, and that of my people at my request; for we have been sold, I and my people, to be destroyed, to be slain, and to perish. If we had been sold as bondsmen and bondswomen, I had held my tongue, although our enemy would never repair the king's loss."

The king asked, "Where is he who dares presume in his heart to do so?"

And Esther said, "The adversary and enemy is this wicked Haman."

Then Haman was afraid. And when the king rose in his wrath and went into the palace garden, Haman knelt down to beg for his life of Esther the queen; for he saw that there was evil determined against him by the king.

When the king returned from the palace garden, and found Haman fallen upon the couch on which Esther sat, he said, "Will he also force the queen before me in the house?" As the words left the king's mouth, Haman's face darkened. And Harbonah, one of the chamberlains, said to the king, "A gallows fifty cubits high, which Haman has made for Mordecai, stands at the house of Haman." Then the king said, "Hang him upon it!"

So they hanged Haman on the gallows which he had prepared for Mordecai.

The king Ahasuerus gave the house of Haman to Esther the queen. And Mordecai came before the king, for Esther revealed what he was to her. The king took off his ring, which he had taken from Haman, and gave it to Mordecai. And Esther set Mordecai over the house of Haman.

Esther spoke again to the king, and fell down at his feet, and besought him with tears to put away the evil decree of Haman the Agagite against the Jews.

Then the king Ahasuerus said to Esther the queen and to Mordecai the Jew, "Behold, I have given Esther the house of Haman, and him they have hanged upon the gallows because he laid his hand upon the Jews. Write now, in the king's name, for the Jews as it pleases you, and seal it with the king's ring; for that which is written in the king's name, and sealed with the king's ring, may no man reverse."

Then were the king's scribes summoned; and it was written according to all that Mordecai commanded, to the lieutenants and the deputies and rulers of the provinces, to each people in their language. And he wrote in the name of King Ahasuerus, and sealed it with the king's ring, and sent letters by posts on horseback, and riders on mules, camels, and young dromedaries, annulling Haman's decree. So the posts hastened and pressed on by the king's command.

Mordecai went out from the presence of the king in royal apparel of blue and white, and with a great crown of gold, and with a garment of fine linen and purple. And the city of Shushan rejoiced and was glad.

The Jews had light, and gladness, and joy, and honor. And in every province, wherever the king's decree came, the Jews celebrated a feast and a good day.

Now on the twelfth month, that is, the month of Adar, on the thirteenth day, the day when the enemies of the Jews hoped to have power over them (though it was turned to the contrary), the Jews assembled together throughout the provinces of King Ahasuerus to lay hands on such as sought to harm them. And the rulers and officers of the king helped the Jews, because the fear of Mordecai had fallen upon them.

On the fourteenth day they rested, and made it a day of feasting and gladness and of sending gifts to one another.

Mordecai wrote all these things down, and sent letters to all the Jews who were in all the provinces of King Ahasuerus, both near and far, that they should keep the fourteenth day of the month Adar, and the fifteenth day of the same, each year as the days which were turned for them from sorrow to joy, and from mourning to a good day; and that they should make them days of feasting and joy, and of sending gifts to one another and gifts to the poor.

And the Jews undertook to do as Mordecai had written to them.

They called these days Purim, for Haman, the enemy of the Jews, had cast the *pur,* that is, the lot, to consume and destroy them, and his wickedness had returned upon his own head. And the Jews ordained, and took it upon themselves and upon their descendants, to keep these two days each year throughout every generation.

And the decree of Esther confirmed these matters of Purim, and it was recorded in the book.

(*The Bible for Family Reading,* pp. 452-59)

Purim Prayer Added to the Daily Service

In the days of Mordecai and Esther, in Shushan the capital, when the wicked Haman rose up against them, and sought to destroy, to slay and cause to perish all the Jews, both young and old, women and little children, on one day, on the thirteenth day of the twelfth month, which is the month *Adar,* and to take the spoil of them for a prey,—then didst Thou in Thine abundant mercy bring his counsel to nought, didst frustrate his design, and return his recompense upon his own head; and they hanged him and his sons upon the gallows.

(O-1, pp. 152-53; cf. *R-1,* p. 298)

FROM THE HOME SERVICE FOR THE EVE OF PASSOVER

The leader lifts up the *matzah* and says:

Lo! This is the bread of affliction which our fathers ate in the land of Egypt. Let all who are hungry come and eat. Let all who are in want come and celebrate the Passover with us. May it be God's will to redeem us from all trouble and from all servitude. Next year at this season, may the whole house of Israel be free!

(R-3, p. 18; cf. *O-4,* pp. 21-23)

The youngest child present asks the following questions:

Why is this night of *Pesah* so different from all other nights of the year? On all other nights, we eat either leavened or unleavened bread; why on this night, do we eat only *matzah,* which is unleavened bread? On all other nights we eat vegetables and herbs of all kinds; why on this night, do we eat bitter herbs especially? On all other nights, we never think of dipping herbs in water or in anything else; why on this night, do we dip the parsley in salt water and the bitter herbs in *Haroset?* On all other nights, everyone sits up straight at the table; why on this night do we all recline at the table?

(Rec-4, p. 15; cf. *R-3,* p. 18; *O-4,* pp. 23-25)

We celebrate tonight because we were Pharaoh's bondmen in Egypt, and the Lord our God delivered us with a mighty hand. Had not the Holy One, blessed be He, redeemed our fathers from Egypt, we, our children and our children's children would have remained slaves. Therefore even if all of us were wise and well-versed in the Torah, it would still be our duty, from year to year,

to tell the story of the deliverance from Egypt. Indeed to dwell
at length on it, is accounted praiseworthy.

(R-3, p. 20; cf. O-4, p. 25)

FROM THE SYNAGOGUE SERVICE FOR PASSOVER

Dew, precious dew, our granaries to fill,
And us with youthful freshness to enharden!
Beloved God, uplift us at Thy will
And make us as a richly watered garden
    With dew.

Dew, precious dew, that we our harvest reap,
And guard our fatted flocks and herds from leanness!
Behold our people follow Thee like sheep,
And look to Thee to give the earth her greenness
    With dew.

(O-3, pp. 187-188; C-1, p. 181)

The home service for the Passover eve in its Orthodox
version is found in innumerable editions of the *Haggadah,*
many of them with English translation, a number of them
illustrated and provided with music for the hymns which are
part of this service. *O-4,* prepared by the Jewish Welfare
Board, in 1943, for distribution to the Jewish personnel in
the armed services, is a book of 147 pages. *R-3* includes many
historical notes and numbers 162 pages. *Rec-4* is an attractive
volume of 172 pages.

The synagogue service for Passover is very similar to that
of *Succot* and may be found in the volumes enumerated in
the notes on *Succot.*

FROM THE SERVICE FOR THE FEAST OF WEEKS

His is eternal power that no words can sufficiently define,
Even were all the heavens parchment, all the reeds—pens,
The seas and all gatherings of water—ink,

And the inhabitants of the earth—writers and recorders.
The glorious Master of the heavens and Ruler of the earth
Alone raised the world and brought it under His dominion,
And perfected it without exertion or fatigue,
With only one light, impalpable sound.
In six days He created and made all His work,
And then the splendor of His Glory ascended on His throne
    of fire. . . .
Exalted is the Lord from the beginning to the end,
Who loved us and graciously gave us His Law.

                     (From *Akdamut—O-3*, pp. 224 ff.
                     C-1, pp. 185 ff.)

With the exception of hymns and *Pityutim,* such as the above selection, the order of service for the Feast of Weeks is similar to that of the Festival of Booths and may be found in the same sources.

INDEX

Ab (month), 76
Ab, ninth of, 73, 109, 125
Abel, 39
Abraham, 3, 4, 9, 34, 39, 41, 65, 79, 114, 115, 118
Academies, 16, 48
Adam, 67
Adar (month), 76
Additional service *(Musaf)*, 49, 220
Adoration, 55, 199
Adult education, 120
Adultery, 13
Afternoon service, 49, 57
Ahasuerus, King, 97, 98
Akiba, Rabbi, 104, 118, 124
America, 21, 30, 33, 36, 89, 90
Amidah. See Eighteen Benedictions
Amram, Gaon, 48
Angel of Death, 99, 100, 129
Animals, prohibited (as food), 134-35
Anniversary of death, 109
Antiochus, 93-95
Apocrypha, 15, 95, 132, 185
Apple, dipped in honey on New Year, 80
Aramaic, 16, 56, 59, 126, 187
Arch of Titus, 139
Ark, 55, 56, 59, 85, 91, 109, 121, 139, 141
Aron Hakodesh. See Ark
Articles of Faith (Thirteen Principles), 5, 6, 7, 60
Arts, 191
Ashkenazim, 19, 21
Assyrians, 3
Atonement, 42
Atonement, Day of *(Yom Kippur),* 40, 49, 58, 73, 77, 79, 82-85, 87, 108, 109, 114, 130, 143, 215, 216
Atonement, Little Day of *(Yom Kippur Katan),* 109
Atonement Day service, 216
Awe, Days of, 77, 87

Babylonia, 3, 16, 21, 45, 47, 48, 75, 109, 110

Babylonian exile, 4, 9
Babylonian Talmud, 16, 18, 187
Bar Mitzvah, 120-23
Barcelona, 47
Bar'hu, 196, 201
Bat Mitzvah, 122
Ben Gurion, David, 36
Benedictions, 52
Bet Yosef, 18
Bethlehem, 107
Bethulia, 97
Bible, 17, 18, 19, 20, 22, 24, 34, 42, 71, 87, 88, 90, 96, 114, 119, 121, 129, 132, 133, 147, 183, 184, 187
Biblical names, 116
Bill of divorcement, 128
Bitter herbs (Passover symbol), 102
Blessing over wine, 71
Blessings, 49
Blessings over food, 50
Blood as food, prohibited, 134
Book of Life, 77, 83, 86, 96
Book of Splendor. See Zohar
Booths, Festival of *(Succot),* 40, 42, 77, 86-91, 141, 218-20
Booths, Festival of, prayers, 218-20
Breastplate, 144
B'rit Milah. See Circumcision
Bureau of Jewish Education, 118
Burial customs, 129

Cabbalah, 19, 144
Cain, 39
Calendar, 75
Camps, 120
Canaan, 88, 107
Candelabra, 139
Candle-lighting service, 221
Canopy. *See* Wedding canopy
Cantor, 59, 126, 214
Captivity, Babylonian. *See* Babylonian exile
Carnivals, 98
Caro, Joseph, 18, 19, 23
Central Conference of American Rabbis, 186

235